Lecture Notes in Computer Scie

Commenced Publication in 1973
Founding and Former Series Editors:
Gerhard Goos, Juris Hartmanis, and Jan van Leeuwen

W. James MacLean (Ed.)

Spatial Coherence for Visual Motion Analysis

First International Workshop, SCVMA 2004
Prague, Czech Republic, May 15, 2004
Revised Papers

 Springer

Volume Editor

W. James MacLean
University of Toronto
Department of Electrical and Computer Engineering
10 King's College Road, Toronto, Ontario, M5S 3G4 , Canada
E-mail: maclean@eecg.toronto.edu

Library of Congress Control Number: 2006922617

CR Subject Classification (1998): I.2.10, I.4.8, I.5, I.3.5, F.2.2

LNCS Sublibrary: SL 6 – Image Processing, Computer Vision, Pattern Recognition, and Graphics

ISSN   0302-9743
ISBN-10   3-540-32533-6 Springer Berlin Heidelberg New York
ISBN-13   978-3-540-32533-8 Springer Berlin Heidelberg New York

Springer is a part of Springer Science+Business Media

springer.com

© Springer-Verlag Berlin Heidelberg 2006
Printed in Germany

Typesetting: Camera-ready by author, data conversion by Scientific Publishing Services, Chennai, India
Printed on acid-free paper   SPIN: 11676959   06/3142   5 4 3 2 1 0

Preface

Motion analysis is a central problem in computer vision, and the past two decades have seen important advances in this field. However, visual motion is still often considered on a pixel-by-pixel basis, even though this ignores the fact that image regions corresponding to a single object usually undergo motion that is highly correlated. Further, it is often of interest to accurately measure the boundaries of moving regions. In the case of articulated motion, especially human motion, discovering motion boundaries is non-trivial but an important task nonetheless. Another related problem is identifying and grouping multiple disconnected regions moving with similar motions, such as a flock of geese. Early approaches focused on measuring motion of either the boundaries or the interior, but seldom both in unison. For several years now, attempts have been made to include spatial coherence terms into algorithms for 2- and 3-D motion recovery, as well as motion boundary estimation.

This volume is a record of papers presented at the First International Workshop on Spatial Coherence for Visual Motion Analysis, held May 15th, 2004 in Prague, in conjunction with the European Conference on Computer Vision (LNCS 3021–4). The workshop examined techniques for integrating spatial coherence constraints during motion analysis of image sequences. The papers were revised after the workshop to allow for incorporation of feedback from the workshop.

I would like to thank the program committee for their time and effort in reviewing the submissions received for the workshop. Further thanks go to Radim Sara of the ECCV 2004 organizing committee for handling the local arrangements for the workshop. Finally, I would also like to gratefully acknowledge the financial support of MD Robotics, Brampton, Canada.

W. James MacLean

Program Committee

Table of Contents

2D Motion Description and Contextual Motion Analysis: Issues and New Models

P. Bouthemy

IRISA / INRIA,
Campus universitaire de Beaulieu,
35042 Rennes cedex, France

Abstract. In this paper, several important issues related to visual motion analysis are addressed with a focus on the type of motion information to be estimated and the way contextual information is expressed and exploited. Assumptions (i.e., data models) must be formulated to relate the observed image intensities with motion, and other constraints (i.e., motion models) must be added to solve problems like motion segmentation, optical flow computation, or motion recognition. The motion models are supposed to capture known, expected or learned properties of the motion field, and this implies to somehow introduce spatial coherence or more generally contextual information. The latter can be formalized in a probabilistic way with local conditional densities as in Markov models. It can also rely on predefined spatial supports (e.g., blocks or pre-segmented regions). The classic mathematical expressions associated with the visual motion information are of two types. Some are continuous variables to represent velocity vectors or parametric motion models. The other are discrete variables or symbolic labels to code motion detection output (binary labels) or motion segmentation output (numbers of the motion regions or layers). We introduce new models, called mixed-state auto-models, whose variables belong to a domain formed by the union of discrete and continuous values, and which include local spatial contextual information. We describe how such models can be specified and exploited in the motion recognition problem. Finally, we present a new way of investigating the motion detection problem with spatial coherence being associated to a perceptual grouping principle.

1 Introduction

Motion is seamlessly perceived by human beings when directly observing a day-life scene, but also when watching films, videos or TV programs, or even various domain-specific image sequences such as meteorological or heart ultrasound ones. However, motion information is hidden in the image sequences supplied by image sensors. It has to be recovered from the observations formed by the image intensities in the successive frames of the sequence.

Assumptions (i.e., *data models*) must be formulated to relate the observed image intensities with motion. When dealing with video, the commonly used data model is the brightness constancy constraint which states that the intensity does not change along the trajectory of the moving point in the image plane (at least, to a short time extent). The motion constraint equation can then be expressed in a differential form that relates

W.J. MacLean (Ed.): SCVMA 2004, LNCS 3667, pp. 1–15, 2006.

the 2D velocity vector, the spatial image gradient and the temporal intensity derivative at any point p in the image. Nevertheless, this enables to locally retrieve one component of the velocity vector only, the so-called normal flow, which corresponds to the aperture problem. Then, other constraints (i.e., *motion models*) must be added. They are supposed to formalize known, expected or learned properties of the motion field, and this implies to somehow introduce spatial coherence or more generally contextual information.

In this paper, several important issues related to visual motion analysis are addressed with a focus on the type of motion information to be estimated and the way contextual information is formulated and exploited. Visual motion information can involve different kinds of mathematical variables. First, we can deal with *continuous variables* to represent the motion field : velocity vectors $\mathbf{w}(p)$ with $\mathbf{w}(p) \in \mathbb{R}^2$, or parametric motion models with parameters $\theta \in \mathbb{R}^d$ with d denoting the number of parameters. Let us note that the latter can be equivalently represented by the model flow vectors $\{\mathbf{w}_\theta(p)\}$ with $\mathbf{w}_\theta(p) \in \mathbb{R}^2$. Second, we can consider *discrete values or symbolic labels* to code motion detection output: binary values $\{0, 1\}$, or motion segmentation output: number n of the motion region or layer with $n \in \{1, ..., N\}$. Furthermore, we will introduce new models, called *mixed-state auto-models*, whose variables belong to a domain formed by the union of discrete and continuous values, and which include local spatial contextual information too. We will describe how such models can be specified and exploited in the motion recognition problem.

Spatial coherence can be formalized by conditional densities defined on local neighborhoods as in Markov Random Field (MRF) models, or equivalently by potentials on cliques as in Gibbs distributions. Another way is to first segment each image into spatial regions according to a given criterion (grey level, colour, texture) and to analyse the motion information over these regions. Perceptual grouping schemes can also be envisaged.

The remainder of the paper is organized as follows. In Section 2, the motion measurements that can be locally computed are briefly recalled and the subsequent needs for complementary constraints or motion models are outlined. Section 3 reviews briefly several MRF-based approaches we developed in the past to deal with the motion segmentation issue stated as a contextual labeling problem involving discrete variables. Section 4 is concerned with the main aspects of optical flow computation using MRF models or more generally relying on energy minimization methods. In that case, continuous motion variables are considered. Motion recognition or classification, and more specifically event detection in video, is addressed in Section 5, requiring the introduction of new contextual models with mixed states. Section 6 describes a new way to address motion detection based on a perceptual grouping principle.

2 Local Motion Measurements

The brightness constancy assumption along the trajectory of a moving point $p(t)$ in the image plane, with $p(t) = (x(t), y(t))$, can be expressed as $dI(x(t), y(t), t)/dt = 0$, with I denoting the image intensity function. By applying the chain rule, we get the well-known motion constraint equation [22, 32]:

$$r(p,t) = \mathbf{w}(p,t).\nabla I(p,t) + I_t(p,t) = 0 \ , \tag{1}$$

where ∇I denotes the spatial gradient of the intensity, with $\nabla I = (I_x, I_y)$, and I_t its partial temporal derivative. The above equation can be straightforwardly extended to the case where a parametric motion model is considered, and we can write:

$$r_\theta(p,t) = \mathbf{w}_\theta(p,t).\nabla I(p,t) + I_t(p,t) = 0 \ , \tag{2}$$

where θ denotes the vector of motion model parameters. It can be easily derived from equation (1) that the motion information which can be locally recovered at a pixel p is contained in the *normal flow* given by:

$$\nu(p,t) = \frac{-I_t(p,t)}{\|\nabla I(p,t)\|} \ . \tag{3}$$

It can also be written in a vectorial form: $\boldsymbol{\nu}(p,t) = \frac{-I_t(p,t)}{\|\nabla I(p,t)\|}\boldsymbol{\omega}_{\nabla I}(p,t)$, where $\boldsymbol{\omega}_{\nabla I}$ denotes the unit vector parallel to the intensity spatial gradient. However, it should be clear that the orientation of the normal flow vector does not convey any information on the motion direction, but implicitly on the object texture (for inner points) or on the object shape (for points on the object border). Besides, the normal flow can be computed at the right scale to enforce reliability as explained in [15].

In case of a moving camera and assuming that the dominant image motion is due to the camera motion and can be correctly described by a 2D parametric motion model, we can exhibit the *residual normal flow* given by:

$$\nu_{res}(p,t) = \frac{-DFD_{\hat{\theta}}(p,t)}{\|\nabla I(p,t)\|} \ , \tag{4}$$

where $DFD_{\hat{\theta}}(p,t) = I(p + \mathbf{w}_{\hat{\theta}}, t+1) - I(p,t)$ is the displaced frame difference corresponding to the compensation of the dominant motion described by the estimated motion model parameters $\hat{\theta}$.

Since the computation of intensity derivatives is usually affected by noise and can be unreliable in nearly uniform areas, it may be preferable to consider the local mean of the absolute magnitude of normal residual flows weighted by the square of the norm of the spatial intensity gradient (as proposed in [23, 36]):

$$\bar{\nu}_{res}(p,t) = \frac{\sum_{q \in \mathcal{F}(p)} \|\nabla I(q,t)\|.|DFD_{\hat{\theta}_t}(q)|}{\max\left(\eta^2, \sum_{q \in \mathcal{F}(p)} \|\nabla I(q,t)\|^2\right)} \ , \tag{5}$$

where $\mathcal{F}(p)$ is a local spatial window centered in pixel p (typically a 3×3 window), and η^2 is a predetermined constant related to the noise level. An interesting property of the local motion quantity $\bar{\nu}_{res}(p)$ is that the reliability of the conveyed motion information can be locally evaluated. Given the lowest motion magnitude δ to be detected, we can derive two bounds, $l_\delta(p)$ and $L_\delta(p)$, verifying the following properties [36]. If $\bar{\nu}_{res}(p) < l_\delta(p)$, the magnitude of the (unknown) true velocity vector $\mathbf{w}(p)$ is necessarily lower than δ. Conversely, if $\bar{\nu}_{res}(p) > L_\delta(p)$, $\|\mathbf{w}(p)\|$ is necessarily greater than δ.

The two bounds l_δ and L_δ can be directly computed from the spatial derivatives of the intensity function within the window $\mathcal{F}(p)$.

By defining the motion quantity $\bar{\nu}_{res}(p)$, we already advocate the interest of considering spatial coherence to compute motion information. Here, it simply amounts to a weighted averaging over a small spatial support and it only concerns the data model. In the same vein, more information can be locally extracted by considering small spatio-temporal supports, either through spatio-temporal (frequency-based) velocity-tuned filters as in [16] or using 3D orientation tensors [4, 33]. On the other hand, more benefit can be gained by introducing contextual information through the motion models.

3   Discrete Motion Labels and Motion Segmentation

One important step ahead in solving the motion segmentation problem was to formulate the motion segmentation problem as a statistical contextual labeling problem or in other words as a discrete Bayesian inference problem [7, 31]. Segmenting the moving objects is then equivalent to assigning the proper (symbolic) label (i.e., the region number) to each pixel in the image. The advantages are mainly two-fold. Determining the support of each region is then implicit and easy to handle: it merely results from extracting the connected components of pixels with the same label. Introducing spatial coherence can be straightforwardly (and locally) expressed by exploiting MRF models.

Here, by motion segmentation, we mean the competitive partitioning of the image into motion-based homogeneous regions. Motion detection can be viewed as a simplified case where two labels only are considered: static background versus moving object, either with a static camera [1, 30, 39], or a mobile one [36]. The latter assumes that the camera motion (or more specifically, the dominant global motion) can be computed and somehow canceled, usually requiring to resort to robust estimation as we proposed in [35] (joint work with Jean-Marc Odobez). This formulation can also encompass the determination of motion layers by assuming that the regions of same label are not necessarily connected [41].

Formally, we have to determine the hidden discrete motion variables (i.e., region numbers) $l(i)$ where i denotes a site (usually, a pixel of the image grid; it could be also an elementary block [7, 13]). Let $l = \{l(i), i \in S\}$. Each label $l(i)$ takes its value in the set $\Lambda = \{1, .., N_{reg}\}$ where N_{reg} is also unknown. Moreover, the motion of each region is represented by a motion model (usually, a 2D affine motion model of parameters θ which have to be conjointly estimated; we have also explored a non-parametric motion modeling in [13], joint work with Ronan Fablet). Let $\Theta = \{\theta_k, k = 1, .., N_{reg}\}$. The data model of relation (2) is used. The *a priori* on the motion label field (i.e., spatial coherence) is expressed by specifying a MRF model (the simplest choice is to favour the configuration of the same two labels on the two-site cliques so as to yield compact regions with regular boundaries). Adopting the Bayesian MAP criterion is then equivalent to minimizing an energy function E whose expression can be written in the general following form:

$$E(l, \Theta, N_{reg}) = \sum_{i \in S} \rho_1[r_{\theta_{l(i)}}(i)] + \sum_{i \sim j} \rho_2[l(i), l(j)] \ , \tag{6}$$

where $i \sim j$ designates a two-site clique. In [7] (joint work with Edouard François), we considered the quadratic function $\rho_1(x) = x^2$ for the data-driven term in (6). The minimization of the energy function E was carried out on l and Θ in an iterative alternate way, and the number of regions N_{reg} was determined by introducing an extraneous label and using an appropriate statistical test. In [37] (joint work with Jean-Marc Odobez), we instead chose a robust estimator for ρ_1. This allowed us to avoid the alternate minimization procedure and to determine or update the number of regions through an outlier process in every region.

Specifying (simple) MRF models at a pixel level (i.e., sites are pixels and a 4- or 8-neighbour system is considered) is efficient, but remains limited to express more sophisticated properties on region geometry (e.g., more global shape information [10]) or to handle extended spatial interaction. Multigrid MRF models [21] (as used in [36, 37]) is a means to address somewhat the second concern (and also to speed up the minimization process while usually supplying better results). An alternative is to first segment the image into spatial regions (based on grey level, colour or texture) and to specify a MRF model on the resulting graph of adjacent regions as we did in [17] (joint work with Marc Gelgon). The motion region labels are then assigned to the nodes of the graph (which are the sites considered in that case). This allowed us to exploit more elaborated and less local *a priori* information on the geometry of the regions and their motion [17]. However, the spatial segmentation stage is often time consuming, and getting an effective improvement on the final motion segmentation accuracy remains questionable. Using the level-set framework is another way to precisely locate region boundaries while dealing with topology changes [38, 39], but handling a competitive motion partioning of the image (with the number of regions *a priori* unknown) remains an open issue in that context even if recent attempts have been reported [11, 26].

Finally, let us mention other recent work on Bayesian motion segmentation, exploring the use of edge motion [42], offering extension to spatio-temporal models [11], or introducing (two-step) hidden Markov measure field (HMMF) models [27]. Tensor voting could also be considered as an implicit way to enforce spatial coherence [34].

4 Continuous Motion Information and Optical Flow Computation

By definition, the velocity field formed by continuous vector variables is a complete representation of the motion information. Computing optical flow based on the data model of equation (1) requires to add a motion model enforcing the expected spatial properties of the motion field, that is, to resort to a regularization method. Such properties of spatial coherence (more specifically, piecewise continuity of the motion field) can be expressed on local spatial neighborhoods. First methods to estimate discontinuous optical flow fields were based on MRF models associated with Bayesian inference [20, 30, 43] (i.e., minimization of a discretized energy function). Then, continuous-domain models were designed based on PDE formalism [2, 8, 25, 46]. Spatial coherence can also be explicitly formulated by first segmenting the image in spatial regions forming the delimited domains where motion models, either dense or parametric ones, can be defined and estimated [6, 17].

A general formulation of the global (discretized) energy function to be minimized to estimate the velocity field $\mathbf{w}$ can be given by:

$$E(\mathbf{w}, \zeta) = \sum_{p \in S} \rho_1[r(p)] + \sum_{p \sim q} \rho_2[\|\mathbf{w}(p) - \mathbf{w}(q)\|, \zeta(p'_{p \sim q})] + \sum_{A \in \chi} \rho_3(\zeta_A) , \quad (7)$$

where S designates the set of pixel sites, $r(p)$ is defined in (1), $S' = \{p'\}$ the set of discontinuity sites located midway between the pixel sites and χ is the set of cliques associated with the neighborhood system chosen on S'. In [20] (joint work with Fabrice Heitz), quadratic functions were used and the motion discontinuities were handled by introducing a binary line process ζ. Then, robust estimators were popularized [5, 28] leading to the introduction of so-called auxiliary variables ζ now taking their values in $[0, 1]$. Depending on the followed approach, the third term of the energy $E(\mathbf{w}, \zeta)$ can be optional. Multigrid MRF are moreover involved in the scheme developed by Mémin and Pérez in [28]. Besides, multiresolution incremental schemes are required to compute optical flow in case of large displacements. Dense optical flow and parametric motion models can also be jointly considered and estimated, which enables to supply a segmented velocity field as designed by Mémin and Pérez [29].

Recent advances have dealt with the computation of fluid motion fields involving the definition of a new data model (derived from the continuity equation of the fluid mechanics) and of a motion model preserving the underlying physics of the visualized fluid flows (2nd order div-curl constraint) as defined by Corpetti, Mémin and Pérez in [9]. A comprehensive investigation of physics-based data models is described in [19].

5   Motion Recognition and Mixed-State Auto-models

5.1   Event Detection in Video and Mixed-State Probabilistic Models

A big challenge in computer vision consists in approaching the "semantic" content of video documents while dealing with physical image signals and numerical measurements. Here, we consider the detection of relevant events (dynamic content). Therefore, we focuse on motion information and we propose new probabilistic image motion models. The motion information is captured through low-level motion measurements so that it can be efficiently and reliably computed in any video whatever its genre and its content. Our approach (joint work with Gwénaëlle Piriou and Jian-Feng Yao [40]) consists in modeling separately the camera motion (i.e., the dominant image motion) and the scene motion (i.e., the residual image motion) in a sequence, since these two sources of motion bring important and complementary information. The dominant image motion is represented by a deterministic 2D affine motion model (which is a usual choice):

$$\mathbf{w}_\theta(p) = (a_1 + a_2 x + a_3 y, a_4 + a_5 x + a_6 y)^T , \quad (8)$$

where $\theta = (a_i, i = 1, \ldots, 6)$ is the model parameter vector and $p = (x, y)$ is an image point. This simple motion model can handle different camera motions such as panning, zooming, tracking, (including of course static shots). To estimate the motion parameters θ, we employ the robust real-time multi-resolution algorithm[1] described in [35]. The motion model parameters are directly computed from the spatio-temporal derivatives of the intensity function. Consequently, the model motion vector $\mathbf{w}_{\theta_t}(p)$ is available at any pixel p and time t. The two components of $\mathbf{w}_{\theta_t}(p)$ are finely quantized, and we build the empirical 2D histogram of their distribution over the considered video segment. Finally, this histogram is represented by a mixture of 2D Gaussian distributions denoted γ^{cam}. The number of components of the mixture is determined with the Integrated Completed Likelihood criterion (ICL) and their parameters are estimated using the Expectation-Maximization (EM) algorithm [40].

The residual motion measurements are given by the $\bar{\nu}_{res}(p, t)$'s as defined in (5). The probabilistic model of scene motion is derived from global statistics on these measurements. The 1D histograms of $\bar{\nu}_{res}(p, t)$ which have been computed over different video segments, present usually a prominent peak at zero and a continuous component part. The latter can be modeled either by an exponential distribution or a zero-mean Gaussian distribution, both restricted to $]0, \infty[$ (since by definition $\bar{\nu}_{res}(p, t) \geq 0$). Therefore, we consider a specific mixture model to represent the distribution of the local residual motion measurements within a video segment with density [40]:

$$f(z) = \varrho\delta_0(z) + (1 - \varrho)\phi_\kappa(z) \ , \tag{9}$$

where z holds for $\bar{\nu}_{res}(p, t)$, ϱ is the mixture weight, δ_0 denotes the Dirac function at 0, and ϕ_κ designates either the (restricted) Gaussian density function with variance $1/2\kappa$ or the exponential density function with mean $1/\kappa$, both with support $]0, \infty[$. Consequently, the proposed model has explicitly two degrees of freedom: ϱ handles the peak at zero and κ accounts for the continuous component of the distribution. ϱ and κ are estimated using the ML criterion. In order to capture not only the instantaneous motion information but also its temporal evolution over the video segment, the temporal contrasts $\Delta\bar{\nu}_{res}$ of the local residual motion measurements are also considered: $\Delta\bar{\nu}_{res}(p, t) = \bar{\nu}_{res}(p, t + 1) - \bar{\nu}_{res}(p, t)$. They are modeled, in a similar manner as in (9), by a mixture model $g(z')$ of a Dirac function at 0 and a zero-mean Gaussian distribution, where z' holds for $\Delta\bar{\nu}_{res}(p, t)$. The mixture weight and the variance of the Gaussian distribution are again evaluated using the ML criterion. The full probabilistic residual motion model is then simply defined as the product of these two models: $h^{res}(z, z') = f(z).g(z')$.

Let us stress the peculiar nature of the probabilistic model introduced in relation (9). The value 0 plays a particular role since it accounts for no motion which is a clear semantic information. We can consider that it corresponds to a symbolic state defined by the discrete value $z = 0$ and that the other state is defined by $z > 0$. Therefore, the variable z takes its value in the set $\{0\}\cup]0, \infty[$. We call such a set a *mixed-state space*.

The event detection proceeds in two steps. The first step permits to eliminate the segments that are not likely to contain the searched relevant events. Typically, if we consider sports videos, we try to first distinguish between "play" and "no play" segments. This step is based on the residual motion only. The second step consists in retrieving several specific events among the candidate segments $\{s_0, \ldots, s_N\}$. Here, the two kinds

---

[1] The corresponding software called MOTION-2D can be downloaded at http://www.irisa.fr/vista/Motion2D.

8   P. Bouthemy

of motion information (residual and camera motion) are required since the combination allows us to characterize more finely a specific event. A residual motion model with density h_j^{res} and a camera motion model with density γ_j^{cam} have to be previously estimated from a training set of video samples, for each type j of event to detect. The label l_i of each segment s_i is determined using the ML criterion:

$$l_i = \arg \max_{j=1,...,J} \prod_{(p,t)\in s_i} h_j^{res}(z_{(p,t)}, z'_{(p,t)}) \prod_{(p,t)\in s_i} \gamma_j^{cam}(\mathbf{w}_{\hat{\theta}_t}(p,t)) \ . \tag{10}$$

More details and results on sports videos can be found in [40].

5.2 Mixed-State Auto-models and Motion Classification

Here, we describe joint work with Jian-Feng Yao and Gwénaëlle Piriou and report preliminary results. The scene motion model (to be learnt from image data) defined above only accounts for global (occurrence) statistics accumulated over both the image plane and time (i.e., over all the frames of the video segment). Obviously, it does not capture how the motion information is spatially (or temporally) organized. In [14, 15] (joint work with Ronan Fablet and Patrick Pérez), we have proposed the design of causal Gibbs models from scale and temporal co-occurrences of quantized motion values $\bar{\nu}$. Here, we will extend the model (9) to take into account spatial interaction between neighbours, and define mixed-state auto-models (to follow the terminology introduced in [3]). We will consider the Gaussian case only, but mixed-state auto-models can be defined as well for any distribution from the exponential distribution family [18].

Let us first rewrite the mixed-state probabilistic model (9) in the following exponential family form:

$$f_\theta(z) = \exp\left[\langle \theta, B(z) \rangle - \psi(\theta)\right] \ , \tag{11}$$

$$\text{with} \quad \theta = (\theta_1, \theta_2)^T = \left(\log \frac{(1-\varrho)\phi_\kappa(0)}{\varrho}, \kappa\right)^T \ , \quad B(z) = (\delta^*(z), -z^2)^T \ ,$$

where $\delta^*(z) = 1 - \delta_0(z)$. Let us note that we can easily recover the original parameters ϱ and κ from the "natural" ones θ_1 and θ_2.

To build our mixed-sate auto-models for the field $(z_i, i \in S)$, we start by considering, as in [3], the family of conditional densities $\mu_i(z_i|\cdot) := \mu_i(z_i|z_j, j \neq i)$, that is the conditional distribution of z_i at a site i given its outside configuration $(\cdot) = (z_j, j \neq i)$. Because of the mixed-state nature of the observations at hand, namely the residual motion measurements, we require that all these conditional distributions are of type defined in (9), or equivalently (11). Let us note that, for each i, the parameters $\theta_i(\cdot) = (\theta_{i,1}(\cdot), \theta_{i,2}(\cdot))$ of the conditional density $\mu_i(z_i|\cdot)$ (here, we use the representation (11)) depend on the spatial context $(\cdot) := (z_j, j \neq i)$. It can be shown [18] that there are vectors $\alpha_i = (a_i, b_i) \in \mathbb{R}^2$ and 2×2 matrices $\beta_{ij} = \begin{pmatrix} c_{ij} & d_{ij} \\ d_{ij}^* & e_{ij} \end{pmatrix}$, such that:

$$\theta_i(\cdot) = \alpha_i + \sum_{j\neq i} \beta_{ij} B(z_j) \ ,$$

or in a more explicit way:

$$\theta_{i,1}(\cdot) = a_i + \sum_{j \neq i} \left[c_{ij}\delta^*(z_j) - d_{ij}z_j^2 \right] \, , \; \theta_{i,2}(\cdot) = b_i + \sum_{j \neq i} \left[d_{ij}^*\delta^*(z_j) - e_{ij}z_j^2 \right] \, .$$

It can further be shown that the joint density of (z_i) is proportional to $\exp(-H)$ where the global energy H associated to the *mixed-state Gaussian auto-model* can be written as follows (with $\mathcal{Z} = (z_1, \ldots, z_{|S|})$):

$$H(\mathcal{Z}) = -\left[\sum_{i \in S} \left[a_i \delta^*(z_i) - b_i z_i^2 \right] + \sum_{\{i,j\}} (\delta^*(z_i), -z_i^2)\beta_{ij}(\delta^*(z_j), -z_j^2)^T \right], \quad (12)$$

provided the parameters of H verify:

(i) for any $\{i,j\}$, $e_{ij} \leq 0$;

(ii) for any i and any part $A \subset S \backslash \{i\}$, $\quad b_i + \sum_{j \in A} d_{ij}^* > 0$,

(in particular, $b_i > 0$ for any i).

We now specify the mixed-state Gaussian auto-model for the 4-nearest neighbour system. The binary clique formed by two neighboring sites i and j will be denoted $i \sim j$. We will further assume that the model is spatially homogeneous, i.e., the model parameters are independent of the site i, but it can be anisotropic (different parameters can be associated to the horizontal and vertical directions). From the development above, there are a vector $\alpha = (a, b)$ and two 2×2 matrices $\beta_k = \begin{pmatrix} c_k & d_k \\ d_k^* & e_k \end{pmatrix}$, $k = 1, 2$, such that:

$$\forall i, j, \quad \alpha_i = \alpha, \quad \beta_{ij} = \beta_1 \text{ if } j = i \pm (1,0), \quad \beta_{ij} = \beta_2 \text{ if } j = i \pm (0,1).$$

This model has ten parameters which have to satisfy the following conditions:

$$\begin{cases} b > 0, & e_1 \leq 0, & e_2 \leq 0, \\ b + 2d_1^* > 0, & b + 2d_2^* > 0, & b + 2d_1^* + 2d_2^* > 0. \end{cases}$$

The parameters of the conditional laws $\mu_i(z_i|\cdot)$ are given by:

$$\theta_{i,1}(\cdot) = a + \sum_{j=i\pm(1,0)} \left[c_1\delta^*(z_j) - d_1 z_j^2 \right] + \sum_{j=i\pm(0,1)} \left[c_2\delta^*(z_j) - d_2 z_j^2 \right] \, ,$$

$$\theta_{i,2}(\cdot) = b + \sum_{j=i\pm(1,0)} \left[d_1^*\delta^*(z_j) - e_1 z_j^2 \right] + \sum_{j=i\pm(0,1)} \left[d_2^*\delta^*(z_j) - e_2 z_j^2 \right] \, .$$

We have applied this new motion model to different types of dynamic video contents (Fig.1). We have used the pseudo-likelihood criterion to estimate the auto-model parameters (with a gradient descent algorithm), and the computed values are given in Table 1.

Mixed-state auto-models can of course involve different kinds of mixed states. It is obviously not limited to one discrete value only, but any finite number K of discrete values $\{\xi_1, \xi_2, \ldots, \xi_K\}$, and pure symbols can be considered too. Any type of continuous

Fig. 1. One image of the considered video sequences (top row: *Highway, Water1, Water2* sequences; bottom row: *Leaves, Tree, Fire* sequences)

Table 1. Estimated parameters of the mixed-state Gaussian (isotropic) auto-model for the dynamic video contents of Fig.1

	a	b	c	d	d^*	e
Highway	-4.91	0.35	2.09	-3.45	0	0
Water1	-4.93	0.06	1.63	-3.19	0.01	0
Water2	-5.14	0.23	1.96	-3.49	0	0
Leaves	-4.86	0.91	2.11	-4.77	0	0
Tree	-4.66	1.89	2.16	-5.45	0	0
Fire	-7.03	0.08	2.5	-3.03	0	0

domains included in $\mathbb{R}^n$ can also be considered. The mixed-state modeling framework introduced in this section should not be confused with the models previously developed either for motion segmentation (discrete labels l and continuous motion parameters Θ) or discontinuous optical flow computation (dense velocity field $\mathbf{w}$ and binary line process ζ), since the latter involve two different sets of variables defined on different set of sites. Here, we are dealing with one set of sites and one set of random variables x with mixed-state values. Several important issues need to be investigated such as the estimation of the mixed-state auto-model parameters, the handling of ML or MAP criteria, or the model selection issue. We also plan to exploit these models in different motion recognition tasks. It could be also interesting to revisit classical motion analysis issues such as motion detection, motion segmentation or discontinuous optical flow computation within that framework.

6   Motion Grouping and Detection of Moving Objects

6.1   Problem Setting

Motion grouping is generally understood as the handling and analysis of multiple moving entities taken as a whole [45]. They may be either disconnected while sharing similar motion (such as flying birds, falling snow) or connected to form an articulated system. Here, we rather intend to revisit basic motion issues by considering perceptual grouping principles. More specifically, we aim at applying the Helmholtz principle ([12]) to motion detection, that is to compute an automatic criterion which ensures that a given region is not still (joint work with Thomas Veit and Frédéric Cao [44]).

Variational motion detection methods (in the sense of separating independent moving objects from background, [24, 30, 36, 39]) paradoxically do not solve the problem of the detection itself: precisely, they enable to locate moving objects at each instant, assuming that one or several moving objects are present. Usually, deciding the presence of independent motion is achieved by hypothesis testing: a model of stillness is tested against a model of change and a decision is taken, for instance, by considering the likelihood ratio of both hypotheses ([1, 30, 24]). Nonetheless, this does not completely solve the decision threshold issue. A system that triggers off many false alarms cannot be efficient. This means that one should be able to explicitly formulate an automatic detection criterion and control the false alarm rate, which in turn can provide with a well-founded confidence measure.

The Helmholtz principle is a general perception law. It was recently applied to image feature detection in [12]. The Helmholtz principle states that an event is perceptible, that is to say significant, if its number of occurrences in a random situation is very small. According to this principle, significant events represent large deviations from randomness. Let us summarize the principle as follows. Entities to be detected are the conjunction of several local observations. We define a background model by assuming that all local observations are independent. By using this *a contrario* assumption, we can compute the probability that a given configuration occurs. More precisely, we call number of false alarms of a configuration, its expected number of occurrences in the background model. We say that an event is ϵ-meaningful if its number of false alarms is smaller than ϵ. ϵ can usually be set to 1 and the method considered as parameter-free.

Let us assume that there is no motion. Then, changes between two images of a sequence are due to noise and possible slight -not significant- changes of the images. We make the hypothesis that this noise (whatever its origin) is uncorrelated. We then consider this as the background model (in the statistical meaning), where no motion detection should occur. Let us assume now that an object is moving. The values of the image changes will increase. But what matters more is that this increase will certainly be very spatially (and temporally) correlated. Thus, if we use this background model, we can compute the probability that the change values increase (even slightly) in a compact region of the image. Because of the whiteness assumption in the background model, this probability is easy to compute. It will be very small in a region with a coherent change, leading to an *a contrario* detection. Here, spatial coherence is exploited in two ways: 1) changes associated with a moving object are supposed to be spatially correlated, 2) the detection criterion must be evaluated over a given spatial region. However, it is not part of the designed model. We do not have a model for a moving region; we only use the background model and prove that a moving object does not conform to the *a contrario* noise model. In other words, the corresponding observation cannot result from a random situation. This approach is valid for sequences acquired by a static camera. It is straightforward to extend it to the case of a mobile camera, if we assume that we can compute and cancel the camera motion.

6.2 Designed Method

The designed motion detection method is fully described in [44] (joint work with Thomas Veit and Frédéric Cao). Its main features only will be described hereafter. The case of a mobile camera is considered. The dominant image motion is represented by a 2D parametric model (affine or quadratic one) and is computed with the robust multi-resolution method [35]. First, a motion observation has to be defined at pixel level accounting for the adequacy to the estimated dominant motion. A first choice could be the Displaced Frame Difference $DFD_{\hat{\theta}_t}(p, t)$. However, in uniform regions (with very low image gradient) the DFD is always small regardless of the adequacy to the dominant motion. On the contrary, along highly contrasted edges, the DFD can be large even if the residual motion is low. A small error in the global motion estimation will be immediately enhanced. Therefore, the observation we use is the normal residual flow magnitude given by $|\nu_{res}(p, t)|$, $\nu_{res}(p, t)$ being defined in (4). A high value of this quantity indicates that the motion of the corresponding point differs from the estimated dominant motion, and is likely to be generated by a moving object in the scene (the points of the image where the spatial gradient is too small are ignored). In order to deal with occlusion, a three-image scheme on images $I(t - 1)$, $I(t)$ and $I(t + 1)$ is considered. Two dominant motions are estimated: a forward one from $I(t)$ to $I(t+1)$, leading to a set of parameters θ_t^{t+1}, and a backward one from $I(t)$ to $I(t - 1)$, leading to θ_t^{t-1}. The resulting quantity considered is now:

$$C_t(p) = \min(\nu_{res}(p, t, \theta_t^{t+1}), \nu_{res}(p, t, \theta_t^{t-1})) \ . \tag{13}$$

To apply the Helmholtz principle, the above-defined motion detection variable $C_t(p)$ and a spatial segmentation are jointly exploited. Each region is tested for conformity with the estimated dominant image motion. The *a contrario* model is specified as follows: the value of C_t is distributed randomly according to its empirical distribution. Moreover, the value at each pixel is supposed to be independent of the values at all other pixels. The *a contrario* model is built upon the empirical inverse cumulative distribution function of the observations C_t:

$$F_t(\mu) = \frac{1}{A} \#\{p/C_t(p) \geq \mu\} \ , \tag{14}$$

where A is the surface of the image counted in pixels. Given a region R, the event of interest E is "for at least k points among the n points of the region, C_t assumes a value larger than μ". The probability of this event according to the *a contrario* model is:

$$B(k, n, F_t(\mu)) = \sum_{i=k}^{n} \binom{n}{i} F_t(\mu)^i (1 - F_t(\mu))^{n-i} \ , \tag{15}$$

i.e., the tail of a binomial law of parameters k, n, and $F_t(\mu)$. Now, the question of how to choose the threshold μ arises. One way to solve this problem is to consider a set of thresholds μ_i, $i \in \{1, \ldots, N_\mu\}$ reasonably sampled. In practice, we take μ_i such that $F_t(\mu_i) = \frac{i}{1+N_\mu}$, i.e., the probabilities $P(C_t \geq \mu_i)$ are uniformly sampled in $[0, 1]$. Now, we can define the number of false alarms (NFA) with respect to motion for a

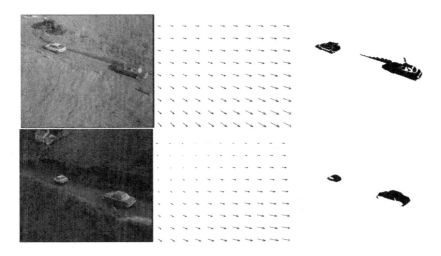

Fig. 2. Sequence "Road" (provided by INA). *Left column:* two original images of the sequence at distant time instants. The cars move leftward along the road. The camera is tracking the cars. *Middle column:* the estimated global dominant motion field is plotted (a 8-parameter quadratic model is used). *Right column:* the detection maps. Cars and associated cast shadows are detected. Detection extends slightly to parts surrounding the dark moving car. NFAs for the left image are about 10^{-10} and 10^{-30} for the white car and the dark car respectively. For the right image, NFAs are about 10^{-4} and 10^{-10} for the white car and the dark car respectively. As demonstrated in this example, detection is effective in quite different illumination conditions.

region R containing n points. For $1 \leq i \leq N_\mu$, we denote by k_i the number of points at which C_t has a value larger than μ_i. The NFA of a region R with respect to motion is defined as follows:

$$NFA_m(R) = N_r \cdot N_\mu \cdot \min_{1 \leq i \leq N_\mu} B(k_i, n, F_t(\mu_i)), \qquad (16)$$

where N_r is the number of regions. We say that R has an ϵ-meaningful motion if $NFA_m(R) \leq \epsilon$. A result is reported in Fig.2. More details can be found in [44].

On-going work is concerned with extending this motion detection scheme to include temporal integration. Besides, we plan to investigate this kind of approach to address other motion analysis issues such as region matching and tracking.

Acknowledgements. I would like to thank Patrick Pérez and Jian-Feng Yao for their comments on this paper, and the contributors (quoted in the text) of the described works.

References

1. T. Aach, A. Kaup. Bayesian algorithms for change detection in image sequences using Markov random fields. Signal Processing: Image Communication, 7(2):147-160, 1995.
2. L. Alvarez, J. Weickert, J. Sánchez. Reliable estimation of dense optical flow fields with large displacements. International Journal of Computer Vision, 39(1):41-56, 2000.

3. J. Besag. Spatial interactions and the statistical analysis of lattice systems. Journal Royal Statistical Society, B, 148:1-36, 1974.
4. J. Bigün, G.H. Granlund, J. Wiklund. Multidimensional orientation estimation with applications to texture analysis and optical flow. IEEE Trans. on Pattern Analysis and Machine Intelligence, 13(8) :775-790, August 1991.
5. M.J. Black, P. Anandan. The robust estimation of multiple motions: Parametric and piecewise-smooth flow fields. Computer Vision and Image Understanding, 63(1):75-104, 1996.
6. M.J. Black, A.D. Jepson. Estimating optical flow in segmented images using variable-order parametric models with local deformations. IEEE Trans. on Pattern Analysis and Machine Intelligence, 18(10):972-986, October 1996.
7. P. Bouthemy, E. François. Motion segmentation and qualitative dynamic scene analysis from an image sequence. Int. Journal of Computer Vision, 10(2):157-182, April 1993.
8. I. Cohen, I. Herlin. Non uniform multiresolution method for optical flow and phase portrait models: Environmental application. IJCV, 33(1):29-49, September 1999.
9. T. Corpetti, E. Mémin, P. Pérez. Dense estimation of fluid flows. IEEE Trans. on Pattern Analysis and Machine Intelligence, 24(3):365-380, March 2002.
10. D. Cremers, T. Kohlberger, C. Schnörr. Nonlinear shape statistics in Mumford-Shah based segmentation. 7th European Conference on Computer Vision, ECCV'2002, Copenhagen, Vol. LNCS 2351, Springer Verlag, 2002.
11. D. Cremers, S. Soatto. Variational space-time motion segmentation. Proc. 9th IEEE Int. Conf. on Computer Vision, ICCV'2003, Nice, October 2003.
12. A. Desolneux, L. Moisan, J.-M. Morel. A grouping principle and four applications. IEEE Trans. on Pattern Analysis and Machine Intelligence, 25(4):508-513, April 2003.
13. R. Fablet, P. Bouthemy. Non-parametric scene activity analysis for statistical retrieval with partial query. Journal of Mathematical Imaging and Vision, 14(3):257-270, May 2001.
14. R. Fablet, P. Bouthemy, P. Pérez. Non-parametric motion characterization using causal probabilistic models for video indexing and retrieval. IEEE Trans. on Image Processing, 11(4):393-407, April 2002.
15. R. Fablet, P. Bouthemy. Motion recognition using non parametric image motion models estimated from temporal and multiscale cooccurrence statistics. IEEE Trans. on Pattern Analysis and Machine Intelligence, 25(12):1619-1624, December 2003.
16. D.J. Fleet, A.D. Jepson, Computation of component image velocity from local phase information. International Journal of Computer Vision, 5(1):77-104, 1990.
17. M. Gelgon, P. Bouthemy. A region-level motion-based graph representation and labeling for tracking a spatial image partition. Pattern Recognition, 33(4):725-745, April 2000.
18. X. Guyon, C. Hardouin, J.-F. Yao. Markovian auto-models with mixed states. Preprint, 2004.
19. H.W. Haussecker, D.J. Fleet. Estimating optical flow with physical models of brightness variation. IEEE Trans. on Pattern Analysis and Machine Intelligence 23(6):661-673, 2001.
20. F. Heitz, P. Bouthemy. Multimodal estimation of discontinuous optical flow using Markov random fields. IEEE Trans. on PAMI, 15(12):1217-1232, December 1993.
21. F. Heitz, P. Pérez, P. Bouthemy. Multiscale minimization of global energy functions in some visual recovery problems. CVGIP : Image Understanding, 59(1):125-134, January 1994.
22. B.K.P. Horn, B.G. Schunck. Determing optical flow. Art. Intelligence, 17:185-203, 1981.
23. M. Irani, B. Rousso, S. Peleg. Computing occluding and transparent motion. International Journal of Computer Vision, 12(1):5-16, 1994.
24. J. Konrad. Motion detection and estimation. in Handbook of Image and Video Processing, A.C. Bovik ed., Academic Press, 2000.
25. P. Kornprobst, R. Deriche, G. Aubert Image sequence analysis via partial differential equations. Journal of Mathematical Imaging and Vision, 11(1):5-26, 1999.

2D Motion Description and Contextual Motion Analysis

26. A.-R. Mansouri and J. Konrad. Multiple motion segmentation with level sets. IEEE Trans. Image Processing, vol. 12, pp. 201-220, February 2003.
27. J.-L. Marroquin, E.A. Santana, S. Botello. Hidden Markov measure field models for image segmentation. IEEE Trans. on PAMI, 25(11):1380-1387, November 2003.
28. E. Mémin, P. Pérez. Optical flow estimation and object-based segmentation with robust techniques. IEEE Trans. on Image Processing, 7(5):703-719, May 1998.
29. E. Mémin, P. Pérez. Hierarchical estimation and segmentation of dense motion fields. Int. Journal of Computer Vision, 46(2):129-155, February 2002.
30. A. Mitiche, P. Bouthemy. Computation and analysis of image motion: A synopsis of current problems and methods. International Journal of Computer Vision, 19(1):29-55, 1996.
31. D.W. Murray, B.F. Buxton. Scene segmentation from visual motion using global optimization. IEEE Trans. on Pattern Analysis and Machine Intelligence, 9(2):220-228, 1987.
32. H.-H. Nagel. On the estimation of optic flow: Relations between different approaches and some new results. Artificial Intelligence, 33:299-324, 1987.
33. H.-H. Nagel, A. Gehrke. Spatiotemporally adaptive estimation and segmentation of OF-fields. 5th Eur. Conf. on Comp. Vis., ECCV'98, Freiburg, Vol. LNCS 1407, Springer, 1998.
34. M. Nicolescu, G. Medioni. Layered 4D representation and voting for grouping from motion. IEEE Trans. on Pattern Analysis and Machine Intelligence, 25(4):492-501, April 2003.
35. J-M. Odobez, P. Bouthemy. Robust multiresolution estimation of parametric motion models. Journal of Visual Communication and Image Representation, 6(4):348–365, December 1995.
36. J.M. Odobez, P. Bouthemy. Separation of moving regions from background in an image sequence acquired with a mobile camera. In Video Data Compression for Multimedia Computing, H.H. Li, S. Sun, H. Derin (eds.), Chap. 8, pp. 283-311, Kluwer, 1997.
37. J-M. Odobez, P. Bouthemy. Direct incremental model-based image motion segmentation for video analysis. Signal Processing, 6(2):143-155, 1998.
38. C. Papin, P. Bouthemy, E. Mémin, G. Rochard. Tracking and characterization of highly deformable cloud structures. 6th European Conference on Computer Vision, ECCV'2000, Dublin, Vol. LNCS 1843, Springer Verlag, 2000.
39. N. Paragios, R. Deriche. Geodesic active contours and level sets for the detection and tracking of moving objects. IEEE Trans. on PAMI, 22(3):266-280, March 2000.
40. G. Piriou, P. Bouthemy, J-F. Yao. Extraction of semantic dynamic content from videos with probabilistic motion models. 8th Eur. Conf. on Comp. Vis., ECCV'04, Prague, May 2004.
41. H. S. Sawhney, S. Ayer Compact representations of videos through dominant and multiple motion estimation. IEEE Trans. on PAMI, 18(8):814-830, August 1996.
42. P. Smith, T. Drummond, R. Cipolla. Layered motion segmentation and depth ordering by tracking edges. IEEE Trans. on PAMI, 26(4):479-494, April 2004.
43. C. Stiller, J. Konrad. Estimating motion in image sequences (A tutorial on modeling and computation of 2D motion). IEEE Signal Processing Magazine, vol. 16, pp. 70-91, July 1999.
44. T. Veit, F. Cao, P. Bouthemy. Probabilistic parameter-free motion detection. IEEE Conf. Computer Vision and Pattern Recognition, CVPR'04, Washington DC, June 2004.
45. Y. Wang, S.-C. Zhu. Modeling textured motion: Particle, wave and sketch. IEEE Int. Conf. on Computer Vision, ICCV'03, Nice, October 2003.
46. J. Weickert, A. Bruhn, N. Papenberg, T. Brox. Variational optic flow computation: From continuous models to algorithms. International Workshop on Computer Vision and Image Analysis (ed. L. Alvarez), IWCVIA'03, Las Palmas de Gran Canaria, December 2003.

Structure from Periodic Motion

Serge Belongie and Josh Wills

Department of Computer Science and Engineering,
University of California, San Diego,
La Jolla, CA 92093
http://vision.ucsd.edu

Abstract. We show how to exploit temporal periodicity of moving objects to perform 3D reconstruction. The collection of period-separated frames serve as a surrogate for multiple rigid views of a particular pose of the moving target, thus allowing the use of standard techniques of multiview geometry. We motivate our approach using human motion capture data, for which the true 3D positions of the markers are known. We next apply our approach to image sequences of pedestrians captured with a camcorder. Applications of our proposed approach include 3D motion capture of natural and manmade periodic moving targets from monocular video sequences.

1   Introduction

Periodic motion is ubiquitous in the physical world, from the oscillations of a pendulum to the gallop of a horse. The periodicity of moving objects such as pedestrians has been widely recognized as a cue for salient object detection in the context of tracking and surveillance, see for example [1, 11]. In this paper we focus on the use of periodicity for a different and, to our knowledge, novel purpose: 3D reconstruction. The key idea is very simple. Given a monocular video sequence of a periodic moving object, any set of period-separated frames represents a collection of snapshots of a particular pose of the moving object from a variety of viewpoints. This is illustrated in Figure 1. Thus each complete period in time yields one view of each pose assumed by the moving object, and by finding correspondences in frames across neighboring periods in time, one can apply standard techniques of multiview geometry, with the caveat that in practice such periodicity is only approximate. In this paper we present this idea and apply it to the problem of estimating sparse 3D structure and dense disparity for walking humans.

The organization of this paper is as follows. We review related work in Section 2. In Section 3 we discuss our approach. Experimental results appear in Section 4, and we conclude and discuss future work in Section 5.

2   Related Work

Periodicity is a kind of symmetry, and as such, its use in recovering 3D information is related to approaches that leverage other kinds of symmetry. An early

W.J. MacLean (Ed.): SCVMA 2004, LNCS 3667, pp. 16–24, 2006.

Fig. 1. Illustration of periodic motion for a walking person. Equally spaced frames from one second of footage are shown. The pose of the person is approximately the same in the first and last frames, but the position relative to the camera is different. Thus this pair of frames can be treated approximately as a stereo pair for purposes of 3D structure estimation. Note that while the folds in the clothing change over time, their temporal periodicity makes them rich features for correspondence recovery across periods.

example of work in this vein is Kanade's method of recovering 3D shape from a single view of a skew symmetric object [9]; more recent extensions of these ideas appear in [6, 4]. The periodicity we are concerned with is temporal; in contrast, spatial periodicity (together with homoegeneity and isotropy) has been exploited in several shape-from-texture approaches, e.g. [5, 14], in which the periodicity pertains to texture elements on the surface of a curved object. While the periodicity of walking humans and animals has indeed been used for other purposes, e.g. pedestrian detection [1], to our knowledge the present work is the first to exploit it for 3D reconstruction.

3   Our Approach

In this section we describe our approach to estimating structure from periodic motion (SFPM). In illustrating the idea, we make use of motion capture (or *mocap*) data from [16]. We provide experimental results on regular video sequences in the following section.

3.1   Estimating the Period

In the present work we specify the period of the moving target manually. A number of approaches exist for estimating the period of a walking figure, e.g. [1]. As our focus is on the reconstruction problem, we have not investigated the use of these algorithms, though we do address the issue of error in the period estimation step in Section 4.

3.2   Multiview Geometry Across Periods

The most elementary configuration for periodic structure from motion is the case of two views separated in time by one period. As is well known from [2, 7], the 3D structure of a rigid object can be estimated up to a projective transformation from two uncalibrated views. The periodic motion counterpart to this is illustrated in Figure 2(a,b), which depicts two 2D views of mocap data spaced apart one period T_o in time.

In this case, the camera is stationary and the walking figure has translated and rotated relative to the camera over the course of the period. These two views correspond approximately to a stereo pair of a particular pose of the walking figure. The reconstruction obtained from these two views is shown in Figure 2(c). Since we are using uncalibrated cameras, the reconstruction is arbitrary up to a 3D homography; our display shows the reconstruction using a least-squares homography estimated using the ground truth marker positions. Alternatively, if three or more views are available, one can employ autocalibration techniques such as [13]. Partial calibration information can also be obtained from knowledge about the scene (see e.g. [8] Ch. 18) or from known properties of the moving target, e.g. that it is a human of a certain aspect ratio.

As is the case in standard structure from motion (SFM), the underlying geometry is only part of the problem: one must solve for correspondences between views before estimating the structure.

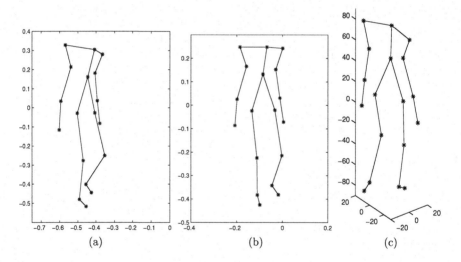

Fig. 2. Illustration of structure from periodic motion using motion capture data: (a) view at time t, (b) view at time $t + T_o$, (c) 3D reconstruction from T_o-separated views

3.3   Solving for Correspondences

In real video sequences, for which identified features are not available as in the mocap data, we can appeal to methods of interest point detection and correspondence recovery that are used in conventional SFM. In particular, we use a RANSAC-based approach [17] on interest points extracted using the Förstner operator [3]. We perform interest point description and matching using the method of [18], which uses the L_1-norm on the error between vectors of filter responses computed at each interest point.

In using RANSAC to estimate the epipolar geometry, we assume that the feature points on the moving object dominate those in the rest of the scene. Because of this simplification, we do not need a separate figure/ground motion segmentation step as preprocessing.

3.4 Computing Dense Disparity

Once the epipolar geometry is known for an image pair, a number of dense stereo correspondence algorithms can be applied along the epipolar lines. In this work we use the method of [10], which is an energy minimization based method using a graph cut approximation. The input to the algorithm is a pair of rectified images (with respect to the object of interest) and the output is a disparity array. For rectification, we use the algorithm described in [8], Sec. 10.12.

4   Experiments

4.1   Walking Person I

Figure 3(c) shows the sparse 3D structure recovered for the T_o-separated frames of a walking person shown in Figure 3(a,b). A detail of the head and left shoulder region is shown in Figure 3(d) from a viewpoint behind the person and slightly to the left. Here we can see that the qualitative shape of the head relative to the sleeve region is reasonable.

The set of points used here consists of (i) the Förstner interest points used to estimate the fundamental matrix and (ii) the neighboring Canny edges with correspondences consistent with the epipolar geometry. Many points appear around the creases in the clothing, but this leaves several blank patches around the lower shirt and the arm.

4.2   Walking Person II

In Figure 4 we show an example of dense disparity estimation for another T_o-separated frame pair of a walking person. The input frames are shown at the top, followed by the rectified image pair. The estimated disparity relative to the left rectified image is shown next; for purposes of visualization, in this figure we have manually masked out the region corresponding to the person. The disparities are shown as a gray level, with lighter shades indicating larger disparity. We observe that the individual's right leg has higher disparity than the left leg, which is consistent with their depth ordering relative to the image plane, and that the majority of the disparity estimates for the rest of the body fall somewhere in between these values. In the original image pair, the light colored top of the forearm bleeds into the bright background; this corrupts the disparity estimate in that region.

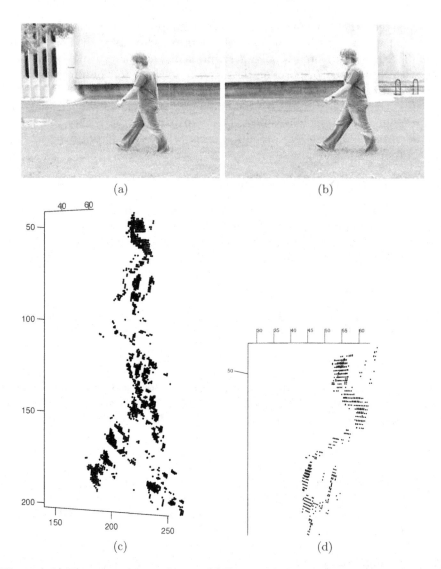

Fig. 3. (a,b) T_o-separated input frames. (c) Estimated 3D structure for interest points. (d) Detailed view of head and shoulder region viewed from behind the person.

4.3   Sensitivity Study

To conclude our experiments, we examine the sensitivity of the 3D reconstruction with respect to errors in the estimate of T_o. For this purpose, we again make use of the mocap data from Section 3.

We consider 200 frames of a regular walking sequence captured at 60 fps with $T_o \approx 90$ frames [16]. Each frame is a 2D projection (cf. Figure 2(a,b)) of the recorded 3D positions (which are accurate to 1mm) of a set of markers rigidly

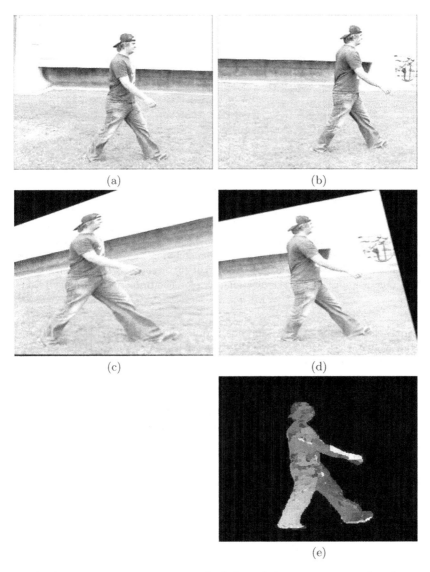

Fig. 4. (a,b) T_o-separated input frames. (c,d) Rectified images computed with respect to estimated epipolar geometry of input frames. (e) Estimated disparity, masked out to show region of interest containing the person.

attached to a subject's body. We selected a different 2D projection of frame 100 as a reference view. Using the reference view together with each of the previously mentioned 200 views, we computed the 3D reconstruction and the root-mean-square (RMS) error relative to the known 3D structure at the reference frame.

The error, which is plotted in Figure 5(a), is computed after solving for the least-squares homography aligning the projective reconstruction with the ground

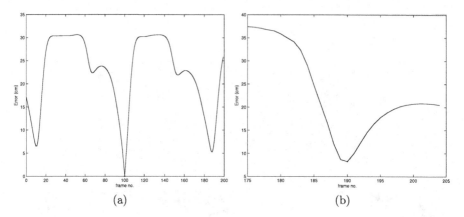

Fig. 5. Reconstruction error vs. frame number for mocap data of a walking person with $T_o \approx 90$ frames. (a) RMS error in units of cm between true 3D coordinates at frame 100 and the estimated 3D coordinates using one 2D view at frame 100 and a different 2D view at each of frames 1-200. (b) RMS error for frames 175-205 relative to frame 100, this time using the same 2D view for the reference frame as for frames 1-200.

truth marker positions at the reference frame. The periodicity is evident in the dips that occur at ±90 frames on either side of 100. As expected, the error drops to zero at frame 100, at which point the reconstruction problem reduces to the case of exact stereo. The plot in Figure 5(b) shows a detail of the reconstruction error computed for 30 frames centered around frame 190; again the reference view is frame 100, but here the cameras specifying the 2D projections are the same for all the views. In each plot, it is evident that the error grows gradually with respect to displacements around the local optimum.

5   Conclusion and Future Work

We have presented an approach to 3D structure estimation based on monocular views of periodic motion. We demonstrated this approach using motion capture data and raw footage of pedestrians. Using the motion capture data, we explored the behavior of the reconstruction with respect to errors in the period estimation step.

The weakest part of the system is currently the correspondence estimation step. In theory, by the definition of periodicity, the problem treated in this work is identical to the classical SFM problem, provided the period estimate is correct. However, in practice, the correspondence problem is at least as hard as the usual stereo correspondence problem, and is in general harder, due to appearance variations across periods. In this regard, the correspondence problem associated with the SFPM problem lies somewhere in between the classical correspondence problem of wide-baseline stereo and the feature correspondence problem in 3D object recognition. We could therefore benefit from the use of methods designed with the latter problem in mind; in future work we will investigate the use of scale-invariant keypoints [12] and affine invariant interest points [15].

Acknowledgments

We would like to thank Sameer Agarwal, Ben Ochoa, and Yi Ma for helpful discussions. We would also like to thank Claudio Fanti and Pietro Perona for providing the human motion capture data. This work was partially supported under the auspices of the U.S. Department of Energy by the Lawrence Livermore National Laboratory under contract No. W-7405-ENG-48 and by an NSF IGERT Grant (Vision and Learning in Humans and Machines, #DGE-0333451).

References

1. R. Cutler and L. Davis. Robust real-time periodic motion detection, analysis, and applications. *IEEE Transactions on Pattern Analysis and Machine Intelligence*, 22(8), 2000.
2. O.D. Faugeras. What can be seen in three dimensions with an uncalibrated stereo rig? In G. Sandini, editor, *Proc. 2nd European Conference on Computer Vision, LNCS 588, Santa Margherita Ligure*, pages 563–578. Springer–Verlag, 1992.
3. W. Förstner and E. Gülch. A fast operator for detection and precise location of distinct points, corners and centres of circular features. In *ISPRS Intercommission Workshop*, Interlaken, June 1987.
4. A. R.J. François, G. G. Medioni, and R. Waupotitsch. Mirror symmetry $\Longrightarrow$ 2-view stereo geometry. *Image and Vision Computing*, 21(2):137–143, February 2003.
5. J. Gårding. Surface orientation and curvature from differential texture distortion. In *Proc. 5th Int'l Conf. on Computer Vision, Boston*, pages 733–739, 1995.
6. A.D. Gross and T. E. Boult. Analyzing skewed symmetries. *Int'l. Journal of Computer Vision*, 13(1):91–111, 1994.
7. R. I. Hartley, R. Gupta, and T. Chang. Stereo from uncalibrated cameras. *Proc. IEEE Conf. Comp. Vis. Patt. Recogn.*, 1992.
8. Richard Hartley and Andrew Zisserman. *Multiple View Geometry in Computer Vision*. Cambridge University Press, 2000.
9. T. Kanade. Recovery of the three-dimensional shape of an object from a single view. *Artificial Intelligence*, 17:409–460, 1981.
10. Vladimir Kolmogorov and Ramin Zabih. Computing visual correspondence with occlusions using graph cuts. In *Proc. 6th Int'l Conf. on Computer Vision, Vancouver*, 2001.
11. Y. Liu, R.T. Collins, and Y. Tsin. Gait sequence analysis using Frieze patterns. In *Proc. 7th Europ. Conf. Comput. Vision*, 2002.
12. D.G. Lowe. Demo software: Invariant keypoint detector. http://www.cs.ubc.ca/spider/lowe/keypoints/.
13. R. Koch M. Pollefeys and L. Van Gool. Self-calibration and metric reconstruction in spite of varying and unknown internal camera parameters. *Int'l. Journal of Computer Vision*, 32(1):7–25, 1999.
14. J. Malik and R. Rosenholtz. Computing local surface orientation and shape from texture for curved surfaces. *Int'l. Journal of Computer Vision*, 23(2):149–168, 1997.

15. Krystian Mikolajczyk and Cordelia Schmid. An affine invariant interest point detector. In *European Conference on Computer Vision*, pages 128–142. Springer, 2002.
16. Y. Song, L. Goncalves, and P. Perona. Unsupervised learning of human motion. *IEEE Trans. Pattern Analysis and Machine Intelligence*, 25(7):814–827, 2003.
17. P. H. S. Torr and D. W. Murray. The development and comparison of robust methods for estimating the fundamental matrix. *Int Journal of Computer Vision*, 24(3):271–300, 1997.
18. Josh Wills, Sameer Agarwal, and Serge Belongie. What went where. In *Proc. IEEE Conf. Comput. Vision and Pattern Recognition*, volume 1, pages 37–44, 2003.

3D SSD Tracking from Uncalibrated Video

Dana Cobzas[1] and Martin Jagersand[2]

[1] INRIA Rhone-Aples, Montbonnot 38334, France
Dana.Cobzas@inriaples.fr
http://www.cs.ualberta.ca/~dana
[2] Computing Science, University of Alberta,
Edmonton, T6G2E8, Canada
jag@cs.ualberta.ca

Abstract. In registration-based motion tracking precise pose between a reference template and the current image is determined by warping image patches into the template coordinates and matching pixel-wise intensities. Efficient such algorithms are based on relating spatial and temporal derivatives using numerical optimization algorithms. We extend this approach from planar patches into a formulation where the 3D geometry of a scene is both estimated from uncalibrated video and used in the tracking of the same video sequence. Experimentally we compare convergence and accuracy of our uncalibrated 3D tracking to previous approaches. Notably, the 3D algorithm can successfully track over significantly larger pose changes than ones using only planar regions. It also detects occlusions and removes/inserts tracking regions as appropriate in response.

1 Introduction

In visual tracking motion information from a video sequence is distilled and unified to determine pose parameters of a moving camera or object. One way of classifying tracking methods is into feature based, segmentation based and registration based.

In feature based tracking a feature detector is used to locate the image projection of either special markers or natural image features. Then a 3D pose computation can be done by relating 2D image feature positions with their 3D model. Many approaches use image contours (edges or curves) that are matched with an a-priori given CAD model of the object [1,2,3]. Most systems compute pose parameters by linearizing with respect to object motion. A characteristic of these algorithms is that the feature detection is relatively decoupled from the pose computation, but sometimes past pose is used to limit search ranges, and the global model can be used to exclude feature mismatches [1,4].

In segmentation based tracking some pixel or area based property (e.g. color, texture) is used to binarize an image. Then the centroid and possibly higher moments of connected regions are computed. While the centroid and moments are sufficient to measure 2D image motion, it is typically not used for precise 3D tracking alone, but can be used to initialize more precise tracking modalities [5].

W.J. MacLean (Ed.): SCVMA 2004, LNCS 3667, pp. 25–37, 2006.

In registration based tracking the pose computation is based on directly align-ing a reference intensity patch with the current image to match each pixel in-tensity as closely as possible. Often a sum-of-squared differences (e.g. L_2 norm) error is minimized, giving the technique its popular name SSD tracking. Un-like the two previous approaches which builds the definition of what is to be tracked into the low level routine (e.g. a line feature tracker tracks just lines), in registration based tracking any distinct pattern of intensity variation can be tracked. Since it's not pre-defined, typically the user points to desired patches in the first frame. This technique can also be used in image alignment to e.g. create mosaics [6]. Early approaches used brute force search by correlating a reference image patch with the current image. While this worked reasonably well for 2D translational models, it would be unpractical for planar affine and projective (homography) image transforms. Instead, modern methods are based on numer-ical optimization, where a search direction is obtained from image derivatives. The first such methods required spatial image derivatives to be recomputed for each frame when "forward" warping the reference patch to fit the current im-age [7], while most recently, efficient "inverse" algorithms have been developed, which allow the real time tracking for the above mentioned 6D affine [8] and 8D projective warp [9]. A related approach [10,11], where instead of using spatial image derivatives, a linear basis of test image movements are used to explain the current frame, have proved equally efficient as the inverse methods during the tracking, but suffer from much longer initialization times to compute the basis, and a heuristic choice of the particular test movements.

In this paper we extend the registration based technique from 2D image plane tracking by involving a full 3D scene model, estimated from the same uncalibrated video, and used directly in the computation of the motion update between frames. Our method starts out tracking the image motion of several surface patches using conventional SSD tracking. After some time (typically ≈ 100 frames) when the scene-camera pose has undergone sufficient motion a 3D model is computed using uncalibrated structure-from-motion (SFM), and from this point the system switches to full 3D tracking of camera rotation and translation using the estimated 3D model. The algorithm does not require com-plete scene decomposition in planar facets, but works with few planar patches identified in the scene. Some advantages of using a global 3D model and local surface patches are that only surfaces with salient intensity variations need to be processed, while the 3D model connect these together in a physically correct way. We show experimentally that this approach yields more stable and robust tracking than previous approaches, where each surface patch motion is computed individually.

The rest of the paper is organized as follows: we start with a presentation of the general tracking algorithm in Section 2, and then present the details for useful combinations of motions (3D models and 2D planar image warps) in Sec-tion 3. A complete model acquisition and tracking system algorithm is descried in Section 4. The qualitative and quantitative evaluation of the algorithm is pre-sented in Section 5 followed by conclusions and a discussion in Section 6.

2   General Tracking Problem Formulation

We consider the problem of determining the motion of a rigid structure through a sequence of images using image registration. A sparse 3D structure for the model described by 3D points $\mathbf{Y}_i$, $i = 1, N$ is calculated in a training stage using uncalibrated structure from motion techniques (see Section 4). The structure points define Q image regions that are tracked in the sequence. Each region $\mathcal{R}_k$ is determined by a number of control points $\mathbf{Y}_{kj}$ that define its geometry. For example, a planar surface region can be specified by 4 corner points. The model points are projected onto the image plane using a projective transformation. First we develop the general theory without committing to a particular projection model and denote the general 3×4 projection matrix for image I_t by P_t. Hence, the model points are projected in image I_t using:

$$\mathbf{y}_{ti} = P_t \mathbf{Y}_i, \quad i = 1, N \tag{1}$$

Let $\mathbf{x}_k = \{\mathbf{x}_1, \mathbf{x}_2, \ldots \mathbf{x}_{K_k}\}$ denote all the (interior) image pixels that define the projection of region $\mathcal{R}_k$ in image I. We refer to $I_0 = T$ as the *reference image* and to the union of the projections of the model regions in T, $\cup_k T(\mathbf{x}_k)$ as the *reference template*. The goal of the tracking algorithm is to find the (camera) motion P_t that best aligns the image template with the current image I_t. A more precise formulation follows next. Refer to Fig. 1 for an illustration of the tracking approach.

Assume that the image motion in image t for each individual model region k can be perfectly modeled by a parametric motion model $W(\mathbf{x}_k; \mu(P_t, \mathbf{Y}_k))$ where μ are 2D motion parameters that are determined by the projection of the region control points $\mathbf{y}_{tkj} = P_t \mathbf{Y}_{kj}$. As an example for a planar region the corresponding 4 control points in the template image and target image t define a homography (2D projective transformation) that will correctly model all the interior region points from the template image to the target image t. Note that the 3D model motion is global but each individual local region has a different 2D motion warp W_k. For simplicity, the 2D warp is denoted by $W(\mathbf{x}_k; \mu(\mathbf{p}_t))$ where $\mathbf{p}_t$ are column vectors of the 3D motion parameters that define the camera projection matrix P_t.

Under the common image constancy assumption used in motion detection and tracking [12] the tracking problem can be formulated as finding $\mathbf{p}_t$ such as:

$$\cup_k T(\mathbf{x}_k) = \cup_k I_t(W(\mathbf{x}_k; \mu(\mathbf{p}_t))) \tag{2}$$

$\mathbf{p}_t = \mathbf{p}_{t-1} \circ \Delta\mathbf{p}$ can be obtained by minimizing the following objective function with respect to $\Delta\mathbf{p}$:

$$\sum_k \sum_x [T(\mathbf{x}_k) - I_t(W(\mathbf{x}_k; \mu(\mathbf{p}_{t-1} \circ \Delta\mathbf{p})))]^2 \tag{3}$$

For efficiency, we solve the problem by an inverse compositional algorithm [9] that switches the role of the target and template image. The goal is to find $\Delta\mathbf{p}$ that minimizes:

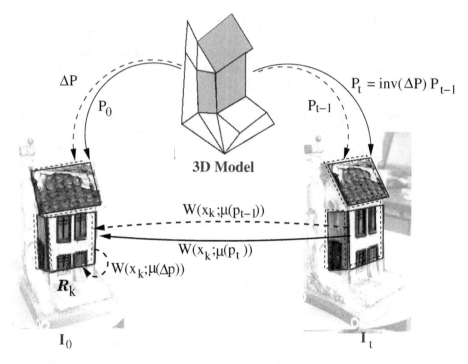

Fig. 1. Overview of the 2D-3D tracking system. In standard SSD tracking 2D surface patches are related through a warp W between frames. In our system a 3D model is estimated (from video alone), and a global 3D pose change ΔP is computed, and used to enforce a consistent update of all the surface warps.

$$\sum_k \sum_x [T(W(\mathbf{x}_k; \mu(\Delta \mathbf{p}))) - I_t(W(\mathbf{x}_k; \mu(\mathbf{p}_{t-1})))]^2 \qquad (4)$$

where in this case the 3D motion parameters are updated as:

$$P_t = \text{inv}(\Delta P) \circ P_{t-1} \qquad (5)$$

The notation $\text{inv}(\Delta P)$ means inverting the 3D motion parameters in a geometrically valid way that will result in inverting the 3D motion, i.e. in the case when $\Delta P = K[R|\mathbf{t}]$ is a calibrated projection matrix, the inverse motion is given by $\text{inv}(\Delta P) = K[R'| - R'\mathbf{t}]$ (see Section 3). As a consequence, if the 2D warp W is invertible, the individual warp update is (see Fig. 1):

$$W(\mathbf{x}_k; \mu(\mathbf{p}_t)) = W(\mathbf{x}_k; \mu(\Delta \mathbf{p}))^{-1} \circ W(\mathbf{x}_k; \mu(\mathbf{p}_{t-1})) \qquad (6)$$

Performing a Taylor extension of equation 4 gives:

$$\sum_k \sum_x [T(W(\mathbf{x}_k; \mu(\mathbf{0}))) + \nabla T \frac{\partial W}{\partial \mu} \frac{\partial \mu}{\partial \mathbf{p}} \Delta \mathbf{p} - I_t(W(\mathbf{x}_k; \mu(\mathbf{p}_{t-1})))] \qquad (7)$$

Assuming that the 3D motion for the template image is zero (which can be easily achieved by rotating the model in order to be aligned with the first frame at the beginning of tracking), $T = T(W(\mathbf{x}_k; \mu(\mathbf{0})))$. Denoting $M = \sum_k \sum_x \nabla T \frac{\partial W}{\partial \mu} \frac{\partial \mu}{\partial \mathbf{p}}$, equation 7 can be rewritten as:

$$M \Delta \mathbf{p} \simeq \mathbf{e}_t \qquad (8)$$

where $\mathbf{e}_t$ represents the image difference between the template regions and warped image regions, and the motion $\Delta \mathbf{p}$ is computed as the least squares solution to Eq. 8.

The derivative images $M = \sum_k \sum_x \nabla T \frac{\partial W}{\partial \mu} \frac{\partial \mu}{\partial \mathbf{p}}$ are evaluated at $\mathbf{p} = \mathbf{0}$ and they are constant across iterations and can be precomputed, resulting in an efficient tracking algorithm that can be implemented in real time (see Section 4).

Computing Derivatives Images

We compute the derivative images from spatial derivatives of template intensities and inner derivatives of the warp. As mentioned before, the 2D motion parameters μ for a region k are functions of the 3D parameters $\mathbf{p}$, the 3D control points $\mathbf{Y}_j$ and the position of the control points in the template image $\mathbf{y}_{0j}$. The projection of the points in the current image $\mathbf{y}_j = P\mathbf{Y}_j$ are mapped to the template image control points through the 2D warp $W(\mu(\mathbf{p}))$ using:

$$\mathbf{y}_{0j} = W(\mu(\mathbf{p}))(P\mathbf{Y}_j), \quad j = 1, N \qquad (9)$$

The warp W is a composed function, and its derivatives can be calculated as:

$$\frac{\partial W}{\partial \mathbf{p}} = \frac{\partial W}{\partial \mu} \frac{\partial \mu}{\partial \mathbf{p}}$$

First the warp derivatives with respect to the 2D motion parameters are directly computed from the chosen warp expression (see Section 3 for some examples). However, the explicit dependency between the 2D parameters μ and the 3D motion parameters $\mathbf{p}$ is in general difficult to obtain, but equation 9 represents their implicit dependency, so $\frac{\partial \mu}{\partial \mathbf{p}}$ are computed using the implicit function theorem. Assume that equation 9 can be written in the form:

$$A(\mathbf{p})\mu(\mathbf{p}) = B(\mathbf{p}) \qquad (10)$$

Taking the derivatives with respect to each component p of $\mathbf{p}$:

$$\frac{\partial A}{\partial p} \mu + A \frac{\partial \mu}{\partial p} = \frac{\partial B}{\partial p} \qquad (11)$$

For a given $\mathbf{p}$ value μ can be linearly computed from equation 10 and then $\frac{\partial \mu}{\partial p}$ is computed from equation 11.

3   Practically Useful Motion Models

Different levels of 3D reconstruction - projective, affine, metric Euclidean - can be obtained from an uncalibrated video sequence [13]. A projective reconstruction gives more degrees of freedom (15 DOF) so it might fit the data better under different noise conditions. On the other hand, fitting a metric structure will result in a stronger constraint, and fewer parameters can represent the model motion (6DOF). For our tracking algorithm we will investigate two levels of geometric models reconstructed under perspective camera assumption - projective and metric. The 3D motion of the model results in 2D motion of the regions $\mathcal{R}_k$ on the image plane.

As mentioned before, the 2D motion is determined through the regions' control points. Different motion approximations are common for the 2D-2D image warps. Warps with few parameters (e.g 2D translation) are in general stable for small regions or simple motion. To better capture the deformation of a region, more parameters should be considered but, in general, tracking with these warps need large surface area or stabilization from a 3D model. A natural parametrization, which also correctly captures motion of planar regions, would be a homography warp for a perspective camera model (projective or Euclidean) and an affine warp for a linear camera model (orthographic, weak perspective, para-perspective). The next subsections give concrete examples of how the tracking algorithm can be applied to three types of useful combinations of motions: an Euclidean model with small translational patches, or larger homography patches, and a projective model with small translational patches.

3.1   Euclidean Model with Translational Warps

A perspective calibrated camera has the following form in Euclidean geometry:

$$P = K[R|\mathbf{t}] \tag{12}$$

where the internal parameters are:

$$K = \begin{bmatrix} a_u & s & u_c \\ 0 & a_v & v_c \\ 0 & 0 & 1 \end{bmatrix} \tag{13}$$

$R = R_x(\alpha_x)R_y(\alpha_y)R_z(\alpha_z)$ represents the rotation matrix and $\mathbf{t} = [t_x, t_y, t_z]^T$ is the translation vector. So the 3D motion parameters are $\mathbf{p} = [\alpha_x, \alpha_y, \alpha_z, t_x, t_y, t_z]$. A translational warp is controlled by one model points for each region and has the form:

$$W(\mathbf{x}_k; \mu) = \mathbf{x}_k + \mu \tag{14}$$

where $\mu = [\mu_x, \mu_y]^T$ is the 2D image translation vector and is computed from the motion of the control point $\mathbf{Y}_k$ using:

$$\mu(\mathbf{p}) = \mathbf{y}_{0k} - K[R|\mathbf{t}]\mathbf{Y}_k \tag{15}$$

The inner derivatives $\frac{\partial W}{\partial \mu}$ and $\frac{\partial \mu}{\partial \mathbf{p}}$ can be directly computed from equation 14,15 without needing the implicit function formulation.

3.2   Euclidean Model with Homography Warps

The image motion of a planar patch can be modeled projectively using a homography warp that is determined by at least 4 control points Y_{kj}. Denote the projection of the control points in the current image by y_{tj}. Note that k is dropped as all the calculations are done for one region. With the Euclidean camera model, $y_j = K[R|t]Y_j$. A homography can be represented using 8 independent parameters $\mu = [\mu_1\mu_2\mu_3\mu_4\mu_5\mu_6\mu_7\mu_8]^T$:

$$W(\mathbf{x}_k;\mu) = \begin{bmatrix} \mu_1 & \mu_2 & \mu_3 \\ \mu_4 & \mu_5 & \mu_6 \\ \mu_7 & \mu_8 & 1 \end{bmatrix} \mathbf{x} = H\mathbf{x} \tag{16}$$

The explicitly dependency of the 2D warp parameters as function of 3D motion parameters is difficult to obtain analytically in this case, but we can apply the method described in Section 2 to compute the inner derivatives $\frac{\partial \mu}{\partial \mathbf{p}}$ using the implicit dependency from equation 9:

$$\mathbf{y}_{0j} = H\mathbf{y}_j \quad j = 1, N \quad (N \geq 4) \tag{17}$$

which can be put in the form of equation 10 $A(\mathbf{p})\mu = B(\mathbf{p})$ with

$$A(\mathbf{p}) = \begin{bmatrix} y_1^1 & y_1^2 & 1 & 0 & 0 & 0 & -y_1^1 y_{01}^1 & -y_1^2 y_{01}^1 \\ 0 & 0 & 0 & y_1^1 & y_1^2 & 1 & -y_1^1 y_{01}^2 & -y_1^2 y_{01}^2 \\ & \vdots & & & & & & \\ y_N^1 & y_N^2 & 1 & 0 & 0 & 0 & -y_N^1 y_{0N}^1 & -y_N^2 y_{0N}^1 \\ 0 & 0 & 0 & y_N^1 & y_N^2 & 1 & -y_N^1 y_{0N}^2 & -y_N^2 y_{0N}^2 \end{bmatrix} \tag{18}$$

$$B(\mathbf{p}) = [y_{01}^1, y_{01}^2, \ldots, y_{0N}^1, y_{0N}^2]^T \tag{19}$$

where $[y_j^1, y_j^2, 1]^T$ are the normalized homogeneous coordinates for $\mathbf{y}_j$.

3.3   Projective Model with Translational Warp

This last example is very similar to the first one except that the 3D motion is represented by a projective 3×4 camera matrix P with 11 independent parameters $\mathbf{p} = [p_1 p_2 \ldots p_{11}]^T$. The 2D warp parameters μ are related to $\mathbf{p}$,:

$$\mu(\mathbf{p}) = \mathbf{y}_{0k} - P Y_k \tag{20}$$

The translational warp is given by equation 14.

This model presents difficulties in calculating a unique and numerically stable inverse of the 3D motion, as required in equation 5. To avoid this problem, while we still compute a global motion update $\Delta\mathbf{p}$ we instead update each warp independently as in equation 6. This solution is closer to the original SSD tracking algorithm [9,8] and, as demonstrated by the experimental results, performs worse than our new algorithm described in Section 2, but still better than the simple unconstrained image plane SSD tacker.

4   Tracking System and Model Acquisition

We incorporated the proposed 3D tracking algorithm is a system that first initializes the 3D model from 2D image tracking over a limited motion in an initial video segment and then switches to track and refine the model using 3D model based tracking. The main steps in the implemented method are:

1. Several salient surface patches are selected in a non-planar configuration from a scene image and tracked in about 100 frames using standard (image-plane) SSD trackers as in [9,8].

2. From the tracked points a 3D model is computed using structure from motion and the stratified uncalibrated approach [13] (projective reconstruction that is upgraded to a metric structure using automatic self-calibration). There are several well known estimation algorithms to recover the projective structure and motion of a scene using the fundamental matrix (2 views), the trilinear tensor (3 views) or multi view tensors for more than 3 views. In our system we used the method developed by Werner et al [14] that estimates the trilinear tensors for triplets of views and then recovers epipoles from adjoining tensors. The projection matrices are computed at once using the recovered epipoles. New views are integrated through the trilinear tensor between the new and two previous views. Assuming that the cameras have zero skew and aspect ratio ($a_u = a_v$ and $s = 0$) and the principal point (u_c,v_c) is approximately known, the Euclidean projections is recovered using self-calibration [15]. There is still an absolute scale ambiguity that cannot be recovered without additional metric scene measurements, but since this scale remains fixed over a video sequence, we can use a 6DOF Euclidean motion model for tracking between frames.

   In a recent paper [16] we compared the accuracy of the SFM algorithms for different geometries (affine, projective, Euclidean) and we show that the model obtained from a scene can be reprojected into new (different from the training) views with a reprojection accuracy of about 1-3 pixels can be obtained (if bundle adjusted). This accuracy is in the convergence range for the tracking algorithm.

3. The 3D model is related to the start frame of 3D tracking using the 2D tracked points y_i and camera matrix computed using camera resection (nonlinear for accuracy [13]) from $y_i \leftrightarrow Y_i$ 2D-3D correspondences. Then the model based tracking algorithm is initialized by computing the derivatives images M at that position. The tracking is now continued with the 2D surface patches integrated in the 3D model that enforces a globally consistent motion for all surface patches.

4. New patches visible only in new views are added by first tracking their image projection using 2D tracking then computing their 3D coordinates through camera intersection in $n \geq 2$ views then incorporate them in the 3D model. In the current implementation the user specifies (clicks on) the image control points y_i that will characterize the new surfaces but in the future we plan to automatically select salient regions.

5   Experimental Results

Two important properties of tracking methods are convergence and accuracy. Tracking algorithms based on a optimization and spatio-temporal derivatives (Eq. 7) can fail to converge because the image difference between consecutive frames I_{t-1}, I_t is too large, and the first order Taylor expansion (equation 7) around $\mathbf{p}_{t-1}$ is no longer valid, or some disturbance causes the image constancy assumption to be invalid.

In the numerical optimization the pose update $\Delta \mathbf{p}$ is computed by solving an overdetermined equation system, Eq. 8. Each pixel in a tracking patch provides one equation and each model freedom (DOF) one variable. The condition number of the linearized motion model M affects how measurement errors propagate into $\Delta \mathbf{p}$, and ultimately if the computation converges or not. In general, it is more difficult to track many DOF. In particular, warp models W which cause very apparent image change, such as image plane translations are easy to track, while ones with less apparent image change such as scaling and out-of-plane rotations are more difficult. A general plane-to-plane transform such as the homography contains all of these and tend to have a relatively large condition numbers. By tracking a 3D model, the convergence is no longer solely dependent on one surface patch alone, and the combination of differently located and oriented patches can give an accurate 3D pose estimate even when each patch would be difficult to track individually.

In Fig. 2 planar regions in the image sequence are tracked using an 8DOF homography. When each patch is tracked individually as in [9] (top images) the first region is lost already after 77 frames and all lost after 390 frames. (See video1 left [17]). The condition numbers for M varies between $5 * 10^5$ and $2 * 10^7$, indicating a numerically ill conditioned situation. When instead the regions are related by the global 3D model using our algorithm, pose is successfully tracked through

Fig. 2. Top: Tracking individual patches using a homography [9]. Not all regions can be tracked through the whole sequence and occlusion is not handled. **Bottom:** Through the 3D model each region motion is rigidly related to the model, and tracking succeeds through the whole sequence. The model also allows detection and removal of occluded regions and introduction of new regions. See video1 [17].

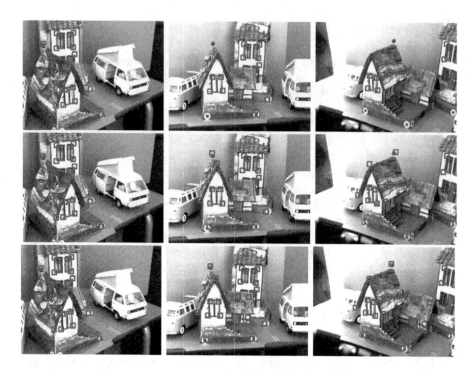

Fig. 3. Top: Translation tracking of individual regions [7,8]. Though the video sequence many patches are lost. **Middle:** A projective 3D model is used to relate the regions, and provide more stable tracking through the whole sequence. **Bottom:** An Euclidean model relates the region, and also allow the introduction of new regions. `video2` [17].

the whole sequence of 512 frames (`video1` right [17]). Additionally the model allows the detection and removal of the region on the left roof side when it becomes occluded and the introduction of three new regions on the right roof side and the smaller outhouse when they come into view. The condition number of the 6DOF (3 rot, 3 trans) model is 900, which is significantly better than the 8DOF homography.

The next experiment uses a simpler 2DOF translation model to relate regions as described in Sections 3.1 and 3.3, through either an Euclidean or Projective global 3D model. In Fig. 3 three cases are compared. In the first, (figure top and `video2` left [17]) no model is is used [7,8], and almost half of the region trackers are lost starting already from frame 80. Because only 2D spatial x and y derivatives are used in M the condition number is very low at an average 1.3. In the middle sequence, a projective model is used to relate the regions. This stabilizes the tracking until about frame 400, where one tracker is slightly off target and further at about frame 430 some are lost due to occlusion. The projective model has 11 DOF and the condition number is quite high at $2*10^4$. In the final (figure bottom) sequence a Euclidean model relates the trackers, and provides handling of occlusions. The condition number is a reasonable 600, and the whole 512 frame sequence is successfully tracked.

Fig. 4. Accuracy experiment. **Left:** Scene image. **Right** current image and template superimposed indicate accurate alignment `video3` [17].

In the final experiment we evaluate the accuracy by tracking four sides of a cube textured with a calibration pattern, see Fig. 4. For each frame we superimpose the warped image onto the template, displaying each using separate color channels. Hence any misalignment can be seen as color bands between the white and black squares. We measured the width of these bands and found that for the Euclidean model with homography warps on average misalignments were less than 1 pixel, and worst case over several hundred frames was 2 pixels. The 3D model will constrain the relative location of the regions, and inaccuracies in the estimated model causes the (small) misalignments we observed. In the case of no 3D model and tracking with homography warps alone the regions would eventually lose track (as in the previous house sequence). But, for the frames when they converged, the alignment was very good, with an error significantly less than a pixel. This is to be expected since the homography parameters allow exactly the freedoms needed to warp planar surfaces into any camera projection.

6   Discussion

We have shown how a 3D scene model, estimated from images alone, can be integrated into SSD region tracking. The method makes tracking of a-priori unknown scenes more stable and handles occlusions by removing and introducing tracking regions as appropriate when new views become available.

In combining different types of 3D global models and 2D region warps we found that:

- Tracking planar regions using an 8DOF homography without a 3D model is unstable due to the many DOF estimated, but limited image signature available from geometric change of only one planar patch.
- On the other hand, using the estimated 3D model we constrain multiple individual patches to move in a consistent way and achieve very robust and stable tracking of full 3D pose over long sequences.

- With some loss in generality and magnitude of maximum trackable pose change, the 8DOF homography can be replaced by simple and faster 2DOF translational trackers. Each individual such tracker has to use only a small image region since it doesn't deform projectively, but instead many regions can be used. Using 2DOF regions and either an Euclidean or projective 3D model this gives almost as good tracking as the homography + 3D model, and makes execution somewhat faster.

Convergence in the last case (translational only warp) over large angular changes in camera viewpoint can be improved by using a few view-dependent templates, each associated with a smaller angular range, and switch these in and out depending on the current angular pose computed from the 3D model. While this introduces a risk for drifts and errors from the templates being slightly offset, in practice we have found it works well using 5-10 different templates over the visible range of a patch.

Visual tracking has many applications in e.g. robotics, HCI, surveillance and model building. Tracking and modeling are interrelated in that (as we have shown) a model improves tracking, and tracking can also be used to obtain the image correspondences needed for a model. In unstructured environments this used to present a chicken-and-egg like problem: Without a model it was difficult to track, and without tracking one couldn't obtain a model. Our method integrates both into a system which is started by defining regions to track in only a 2D image. First 2D tracking is used over an initial video segment with moderate pose change to obtain point correspondences and build a 3D model from image data. After the model is built the system switches to 3D tracking and is now ready to handle large pose changes and provide full 3D pose (rotation, translation) tracking.

A main feature of our method is that 3D pose change ΔP is computed directly from image intensity derivatives w.r.t. P. Note that this guarantees the best 3D pose update available from the linearized model (here using L_2 norm, but other e.g. robust norms are also possible[8]). This is unlike the more common approach of first tracking 2D image correspondences, and then computing a 3D pose from points, where first each 2D point location is committed to based on a locally optimal image fit but without regards to the global 3D constraints.

References

1. Lowe, D.: Fitting parameterized three-dimensional models to images. PAMI **13** (1991) 441–450
2. Marchand, E., Bouthemy, P., Chaumette, F.: A 2d-3d model-based approach to real-time visual tracking. IVC **19** (2001) 941–955
3. Drummond, T., Cipolla, R.: Real-time visual tracking of complex structures. PAMI **24** (2002) 932–946
4. Armstrong, M., Zisserman, A.: Robust object tracking. In: Second Asian Conference on Computer Vision. (1995) 58–62
5. Toyama, K., Hager, G.: Incremental focus of attention for robust vision-based tracking. IJCV **35** (1999) 45–63

6. Szeliski, R.: Video mosaics for virtual environments. IEEE Computer Graphics and Applications (1996) 22–30
7. Lucas, B., Kanade, T.: An iterative image registration technique with an application to stereo vision. In: Int. Joint Conf. on Artificial Intelligence. (1981)
8. Hager, G., Belhumeur, P.: Efficient region tracking with parametric models of geometry and illumination. PAMI **20** (1998) 1025–1039
9. Baker, S., Matthews, I.: Lucas-Kanade 20 Years On: A Unifying Framework. Technical Report CMU-RITR02-16 (2002)
10. Jurie, F., Dhome, M.: Hyperplane approximation for template matching. PAMI **24** (2002) 996–1000
11. Gleicher, M.: Projective registration with difference decomposition. In: CVPR97. (1997) 331–337
12. Horn, B.: Computer Vision. MIT Press, Cambridge, Mass. (1986)
13. Hartley, R.I., Zisserman, A.: Multiple View Geometry in Computer Vision. Cambridge University Press (2000)
14. T.Werner, T.Pajdla, M.Urban: Practice of 3d reconstruction from multiple uncalibrated unorganized images. In: Czech Pattern Recognition Workshop. (2000)
15. Triggs, W.: Auto-calibration and the absolute quadric. In: CVRP. (1997) 609–614
16. Cobzas, D., Jagersand, M.: A comparison of viewing geometries for augmented reality. In: Proc. of Scandinavian Conference on Image Analysis (SCIA 2003). (2003)
17. line mpeg movies of the experiments are available. See `videoX` at http:// www.cs.ualberta.ca/ dana/Movies

Comparison of Edge-Driven Algorithms for Model-Based Motion Estimation

Hendrik Dahlkamp, Artur Ottlik, and Hans-Hellmut Nagel

Institut für Algorithmen und Kognitive Systeme (IAKS),
Universität Karlsruhe (TH), 76128 Karlsruhe, Germany
nagel@iaks.uni-karlsruhe.de

Abstract. 3D-model-based tracking offers one possibility to explicate the manner in which spatial coherence can be exploited for the analysis of image sequences. Two seemingly different approaches towards 3D-model-based tracking are compared using the same digitized video sequences of road traffic scenes. Both approaches rely on the evaluation of grey-value discontinuities, one based on a hypothesized probability distribution function for step-discontinuities in the vicinity of model-segments, the other one based on extraction of Edge Elements (EEs) and their association to model-segments. The former approach could be considered to reflect a stronger spatial coherence assumption because the figure-of-merit function to be optimized collects evidence from all greyvalue discontinuities within a tolerance region around visible model segments. The individual association of EEs to model-segments by the alternative approach is based on a distance function which combines differences in position and orientation, thereby taking into account the gradient direction as well as the location of a local gradient maximum in gradient direction.

A detailed analysis of numerous vehicles leads to the preliminary conclusion that both approaches have different strengths and weaknesses. It turns out that the effects of how greyvalue discontinuities are taken into account are in general less important than the inclusion of Optical Flow (OF) estimates during the update-step of the current state vector for a body to be tracked. OF estimates are evaluated only within the area of the body to be tracked when projected into the image plane according to the current state estimate. Subtle effects related to simplifications and approximations during the implementation of an approach thus may influence the aggregated result of tracking numerous vehicles even in the case where spatial coherence appears to be rigorously exploited.

1 Introduction

Obviously, spatiotemporal coherence plays an important role in human visual perception. Exploitation of spatiotemporal coherence thus offers itself for Computer Vision (CV) although it is by no means evident how to do this, in particular if an 'optimal' use is postulated as an additional requirement. The latter postulate implies that alternative means are compared regarding how to exploit

W.J. MacLean (Ed.): SCVMA 2004, LNCS 3667, pp. 38–50, 2006.
© Springer-Verlag Berlin Heidelberg 2006

spatiotemporal coherence in CV. With the advent of solid-state video cameras, sufficient bandwidth into and out of memory, large cheap memories, and powerful processors, recording and processing of entire image sequences constitutes today's challenge rather than that of single image frames. The concept of an image sequence implies already some kind of temporal coherence. Unless explicitly mentioned, its exploitation will not be discussed separately in what follows.

One of the alternatives with respect to exploitation of spatial coherence involves the question whether this aspect enters explicitly into the approach to be studied or only implicitly. We selected the first alternative. In a second step, one then has to decide whether the approach comprises only representations in the 2D image plane or relies on 3D models for objects of interest in the 3D scene. Examples for explicitly taking into account spatial coherence in a 2D image plane approach are provided by [1] and [4].

The use of 3D models for bodies and their movements in the depicted scene usually involves more complicated algorithms and thus more computing power and/or time, but has the advantage that size variations and occlusion effects can be taken into account in a more 'natural' manner. Spatial coherence in the image plane then is the consequence of models for the camera, the objects, and their movements rather than a postulate for image regions.

Unless considerable prior knowledge about the depicted scene and its temporal development is available, however, a 3D model-based approach necessitates an initialisation phase which either is based on a – potentially quite involved – search or substitutes assumptions for search. Such assumptions usually comprise some kind of spatial coherence. Once the image of a body has been detected, its tracking becomes much simpler based on the postulate of temporal coherence. Experience has shown that object tracking can depend critically on the initialisation phase. Tracking results are thus used frequently in order to assess the initialisation phase, its underlying assumptions and parameterisations. Such an approach implies, however, that the tracking process itself is fairly robust. The desire to exploit tracking results in order to study the complex initialisation phase and its implicit assumptions about spatial coherence thus leads to efforts to clarify the effects of various factors on tracking itself. As a consequence of these considerations, this contribution compares two different model-based approaches for tracking road vehicles, using different traffic videos.

In the next section, we sketch the differences between the two approaches and discuss expected relations between properties of the alternatives and results obtained by each alternative. Section 3 discusses experimental results. Section 4 includes results obtained by an extended approach which comprises Optical Flow (OF) estimates within the image of a body to be tracked, exploiting a different manifestation of spatial coherence observable in the image plane.

2   Discussion of the Algorithms to Be Compared

Both approaches to be compared rely on the evaluation of greyvalue discontinuities. The one reported in [5,6] is based on a hypothesized probability distribution function for step-discontinuities in the vicinity of model-segments. This approach will be referred to in the sequel as 'Expectation Maximisation Contour Algorithm (EMCA)'. The other one is based on extraction of Edge Elements (EEs) and their association to model-segments (see, e. g., [3]). It will be referred to by 'Edge Element Association Algorithm (EEAA)'. In order to facilitate a self-contained discussion, essential aspects of both approaches have been outlined in Appendix A.

Several components are common during edge-based tracking. Their use, however, differs in the two analyzed algorithms:

– Use of *gaussian convolution*: While EMCA convolves the probability distribution for the greyvalue discontinuity position by a gaussian, EEAA convolves the image greyvalues directly. Therefore, EMCA use the gaussian to smooth its figure-of-merit function while EEAA increases the quality of its features, i. e. edge elements.

– Use of *edge intensity*: EMCA includes edge intensity in its figure-of-merit function. To be more specific, the figure-of-merit function is an exponential of the square root of the edge intensity, which can be seen by inserting equ. (2) into equ. (5) and equ. (5) into equ. (10). As the algorithm maximizes equ. (10), the gain of minimizing $\|\boldsymbol{\nu}_{k,j} - \boldsymbol{\mu}_k\|$ is larger if the edge intensity of measure point $\boldsymbol{\nu}_{k,j}$ is larger. In equation (11), however, every sample point is weighted the same, independent of its largest orthogonal greyvalue difference. Therefore, it can be said that the EM Contour Algorithm does not weight the influence of the sample points with their edge intensity. The figure-of-merit function contains such a weighting but the intermediate maximization goal given by equ. (10) does not. The estimation accuracy of the discontinuity location $\hat{\nu}_k$ definitely depends on the edge intensity, as shown in [2, appendix B.1]. EEAA weights its distance measure between edge element and closest projected model segment by the edge element intensity, normalized to the strongest intensity of the vehicle.

– Use of *edge direction*: While EEAA includes the orientation difference between EE and projected model segment, EMCA computes the greyvalue difference in the direction obtained from the model.

– *locality of decisions*: Obviously, it is desirable for an algorithm to avoid making decisions based on local greyvalue structure, because smaller structures are more susceptible to noise than the entire vehicle image. EMCA contains no local decisions in the figure-of-merit function. EEAA decides locally where to put edge elements and where to map them onto the model. Given large filter masks, local EE computation is stable enough but mapping can produce significant jumps in the figure-of-merit function even if the model moves only very little.

In summary, EEAA extracts few, reliable features but can be expected to have trouble associating them to model-segments while EMCA uses many simple features and can be expected to have trouble with their accuracy and fusion.

3   Experiments with Edge-Based Approaches

First, we applied EMCA to the PETS2000 sequence [8] which was used to introduce the algorithm. The results, as displayed in Fig. 1, show successful tracking of all 3 vehicles if vehicles are initialized interactively, vehicle models are assigned individually, and the same parameters are used as introduced in [5]. Using a single model without wheelarches for all three vehicles yields similar results except for wrong directional estimates of the second vehicle. The results are essentially compatible with those reported in [5].

Fig. 1. Tracking results on the PETS2000 image sequence: The first four images show tracking for individually assigned vehicle models at the given frame times. The lower two images show results obtained with the *same* model for all vehicles.

We then compared the performance of both algorithms on the more challenging dt_passat03 sequence [7] displayed in Fig. 2. This sequence contains more vehicles of significantly smaller size than in the PETS2000 sequence. The results obtained with EEAA are essentially compatible with those reported in [3].

Fig. 2. Overview of the dt_passat03 image sequence at frame 953. The vehicles at the traffic light are standing and, therefore, have not been tracked yet.

Figure 3 contains the tracking results showing visibility duration for each vehicle and the period during which the algorithms managed to track it. It can be seen that the EEA-approach scores better than the EMC-approach in a majority of cases, as represented by longer tracking duration until the vehicle is lost.

For a closer examination of the results, Figure 4 contains an exemplary look at two vehicles. The first one (upper left) is partially occluded by a leafless tree which darkens about a third of the vehicle pixels. For EMCA, this results in some mispredicted border positions but the errors cancel out and we are left with a successful prediction. The center left part of Fig. 4 demonstrates this by plotting the figure-of-merit function given by equ. (10) against vehicle displacement in the scene parallel and orthogonal to the vehicle orientation. The lower left part of Fig. 4 depicts the edge elements of the same image part. Because of the random placement of tree branches, these edge elements are very disturbed and mapping to model segments becomes practically arbitrary so the vehicle is lost. EMCA, therefore, performs systematically better than EEAA in cases where the tracked vehicle is occluded by many small objects. The second image (on the right) shows a dark grey vehicle in front of only slightly brighter background. Due to the dependence on the clear distinction between on-border and off-border

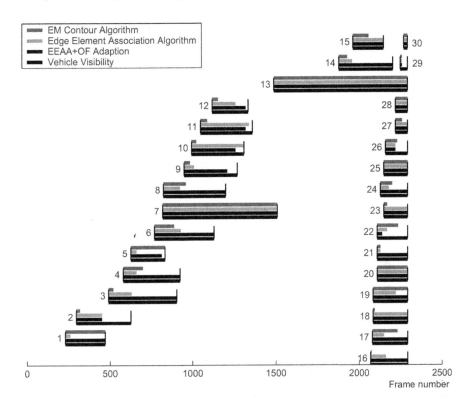

Fig. 3. Tracking results for the dt_passat03 sequence. For each vehicle, four bars show its duration of visibility and duration of succesful tracking using different approaches. From top bar to bottom bar: duration of tracking with EMCA (red), tracking with EEAA (green), tracking with a combination (see Section 4) of EEAA and OF adaption (blue), vehicle's visibility (black) in the image sequence.

greyvalue differences, EMCA fails during the first few tracking frames. As shown in the center right part of the image, this tracking failure can be attributed to its figure-of-merit function plot having a maximum off the center. EEAA performs better in this case as the global edge intensity is not important. The lack of visual appearance of some model edges is irrelevant for EEAA as long as there are at least a few features present.

4   Supplemental Experiments Including OF Estimates

So far, only the exploitation of greyvalue transitions has been discussed. One of the two approaches to be compared offers an additional option, namely the inclusion of OF estimates into the state vector update step. Results presented, for example, in [3] support the expectation that the inclusion of OF estimates considerably stabilizes the tracking process. OF estimates directly influence the velocity estimate in the state vector. In addition, the number of OF vectors which

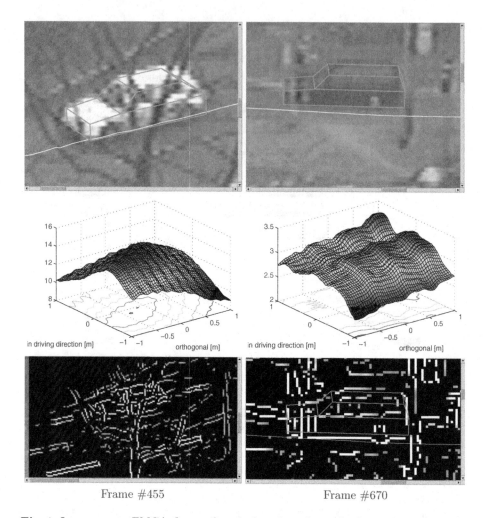

Frame #455   Frame #670

Fig. 4. Image zoom, EMCA figure-of-merit function plot and edge elements for two vehicles of the `dt_passat03` sequence

can be taken into account during the state update is proportional to the area of the projected model whereas the number of EEs is more closely proportional to its boundary length and thus smaller.

As can be seen in Figure 3, the combined EEAA and OF adaption outperforms both other algorithms, especially for the vehicles which drive from the right hand side of the image to the upper side (i. e. vehicle number 3, 4, 6, 8, and 14; with the exception of vehicles 2 and 15 which are tracked equally well by the EEA-approach). Their trajectory includes a right-turn within an area with both lane markers and partial occlusions by traffic lights. Such situations constitute a significant challenge for edge-based algorithms. This structured background, however, helps to estimate Optical Flow correctly, so the combined algorithm can at least estimate speed and direction of the vehicles in this area which is enough to bridge tracking until edge estimation works reliably again. It can be assumed that a combination of EMCA and OF adaption would perform similarly.

5   Discussion and Conclusions

Both the EMC and the EEA approach rely solely on greyvalue discontinuities for 3D model-based tracking. The EMC approach hypothesizes a probability distribution function (pdf) for greyvalue discontinuities in the vicinity of model-segments resulting from the projection of a 3D body model into the image plane according to the current pose estimate. This pdf determines the probability to find greyvalue discontinuities in the vicinity of a model projection. An expectation maximisation step (re-)estimates corrections to the pose parameters in order to maximize this figure-of-merit.

A weakness of the EEA approach becomes particularly discernible in cases where the number of EEs is small such that any incorrect associations between EEs and model-segments begin to distort the pose parameter update step. Another difficulty for the EEA approach is presented by heavily textured image regions with many EEs whose orientation accidentally matches that of model-segments within a given tolerance. It is here where the *local* restriction for EE association with a given model-segment appears to work against this approach, despite the fact that the orientation difference is taken into account explicitly. This observation suggests to reconsider the manner in which position and orientation information of each EE is combined into a compound distance function between an EE and a model-segment. It should be noted, however, that the number of cases where this effect begins to endanger the tracking performance appears to be small with the result that the EEA approach performs still better than the EMC approach. The statistics are not yet large enough, however, to proclaim a clear superiority of one approach over the other. In addition, attention has to be drawn to the fact that no efforts have been made to optimize *either* parameter-set for the implementation used in these experiments beyond copying values available from original publications.

In general, our experiments support the hypothesis that the incorporation of OF-estimates into the tracking phase is more important than the particularities of how EEs are taken into account. This finding is compatible with statements which can be found, e. g., in [3]. One may now argue '... the integration of optical flow information significantly improves the tracking result, which is logic and expected. Such a study does not result in new understanding of the algorithms and most of the results can be predicted'. An analogous critique could be formulated like '... the difference between the two approaches being compared is small compared to the benefits of adding a new source of information from the optical flow. This weakens the importance of the original comparison.'

It is admitted freely that the comparison may be statistically weak, despite the fact that the second image sequence comprises about ten times the number of vehicles than the PETS-2000 sequence, not to mention the differences in vehicle movements and recording conditions. The *experimental* evidence is *significant* that the difference between the two approaches with respect to handling greyvalue transition information appears to be small compared to the effect of incorporating optical flow estimates into the state-vector update. There does not yet exist an accepted theory in this field, however, which would allow *to derive* such a conclusion. 'Hunches' may vary from scientist to scientist or from group to group. Such an observation should not distract, though, from the fact that more attention has to be paid to the manner in which information from greyvalue discontinuities is exploited by the tracking process. Even if such effects may become relevant only rarely during the tracking phase, a negative effect caused by an inappropriate handling of greyvalue transition information can disrupt the tracking process and thereby endanger efforts to maintain the identity of a body moving within the scene.

It is unclear to which extent the consequences of unavoidable simplifications counteract theoretically appealing advantages of alternative approaches. Such a question can only be answered by careful comparative experiments of the kind reported here which – according to the authors' knowledge – constitute by no means the standard manner of research in the field of model-based tracking. A re-appraisal of our original assessment suggests the following conclusions:

1. Comparison experiments, which do not simply reproduce earlier ones under identical conditions, are necessary *even if they largely confirm prior expectations*. The field does not command a proven and accepted theory which allows to predict the outcome of an experiment beyond reasonable doubt.
2. Given the small margin in the currently reported experiments, we refrain from making any final decisions regarding superiority of one approach over the other.
3. Handling of greyvalue transition information during model-based tracking can become crucial in some cases, but need not determine the outcome in general. It thus is not easy to investigate which approach (in which implementation and with which parameterisation) is superior to which alternatives. This observation suggests that larger test samples need to be evaluated, implying a *substantial* increase of efforts to perform such experiments.
4. In addition to the preparation of experimental runs with a larger number of vehicles, other aspects have to be investigated which might potentially influence the outcome of such experiments, e. g., details of the vehicle and/or motion model.
5. If the difference of alternative ways to handle the greyvalue transition information appears to be small, *all* potentially relevant influences have to be uncovered and investigated, including theoretical simplifications and numerical effects.
6. True progress towards better understanding model-based tracking thus appears to be more expensive in terms of eperimental expertise and theoretical analysis than has been anticipated by many in the field.

Additional experiments have been prepared in order to answer at least some of the new questions raised.

Acknowledgments

The authors gratefully acknowledge clarifying discussions with A.E.C. Pece and stimulating remarks by the reviewers. These investigations have been partially supported by the European Union (FP5-project 'CogViSys', IST-2000-29404).

References

1. T. Brox, M. Rousson, R. Deriche, and J. Weickert: *Unsupervised Segmentation Incorporating Color, Texture, and Motion*. In: Proc. 10th International Conference on Computer Analysis of Images and Patterns CAIP'03, 25-27 August 2003, Groningen, The Netherlands. LNCS 2756, pp. 353–360, Springer-Verlag: Berlin·Heidelberg·New York/NY 2003.
2. H. Dahlkamp: *Untersuchung eines Erwartungswert-Maximierung (EM)-Kontur-Algorithmus zur Fahrzeugverfolgung* (in German). Diplomarbeit, Institut für Algorithmen und Kognitive Systeme, Fakultät für Informatik der Universität Karlsruhe (TH), Januar 2004.
3. M. Haag and H.-H. Nagel: *Combination of Edge Element and Optical Flow Estimates for 3D-Model-Based Vehicle Tracking in Traffic Image Sequences*. International Journal of Computer Vision 35:3 (1999) 295-319.
4. N. Paragios and R. Deriche: *Geodesic active regions: a new paradigm to deal with frame partition problems in computer vision*. Journal of Visual Communication and Image Representation, Special Issue on Partial Differential Equations in Image Processing, Computer Vision and Computer Graphics, (March/June 2002) 249-268.
5. A.E.C. Pece and A.D. Worrall: *Tracking with the EM Contour Algorithm*. Proceedings of the 7th European Conference on Computer Vision 2002 (ECCV2002), 28-30 May 2002, Copenhagen, Denmark. Springer LNCS 2350, pp. 3-17.
6. A.E.C. Pece: *The Kalman-EM Contour Tracker*. Proceedings of the 3rd Workshop on Statistical and Computational Theories of Vision (SCTV 2003), 12 October 2003, Nice, France.
7. http://i21www.ira.uka.de/image_sequences/
8. ftp://pets2001.cs.rdg.ac.uk/PETS2000/test_images/

A   Outline of the Two Algorithms

A.1   Edge Element Association Algorithm

During edge element adaption, a new state is searched which minimizes the distance between edge elements and projected model segments. An edge element $\mathbf{e} = (u_e, v_e, \phi_e)^T$ represents a local maximum of the gradient norm in gradient direction ϕ_e at the position (u_e, v_e). As illustrated in Figure 5, the difference measure between an edge element $\mathbf{e}$ and a projected model segment $\mathbf{m}$ considers both the Euclidean distance and the difference between the measured and predicted gradient direction:

$$d_{\mathbf{m}}(\mathbf{e}, \mathbf{x}) = \frac{b}{\cos \Delta}$$
$$= \frac{-(u_e - u_m)\sin\theta + (v_e - v_m)\cos\theta}{\cos(\phi_e - (\theta + \frac{\pi}{2}))} \quad . \tag{1}$$

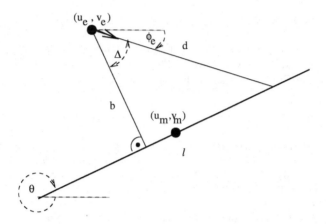

Fig. 5. Distance metric between an edge element and a projected model segment

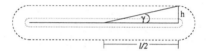

Fig. 6. Region of a model segment in which edge elements are accepted. This acceptance region is specified based on the length of (the visible part of) the model segment.

It is assumed that d_m is normally distributed with zero-mean and variance σ^2. The distance measure induces a Mahalanobis distance which follows a $\chi^2(1)$ distribution. Edge elements which exceed the $(1-\alpha)$ quantile of the Mahalanobis distance are rejected. Edge elements which can be assigned to several model segments are assigned to the segment with the smallest Mahalanobis distance. Furthermore, only those edge elements within an acceptance area around visible model segments are taken into account (see Figure 6).

A.2   Expectation Maximisation Contour Algorithm

According to the publication [5], the assumptions underlying this algorithm are

1. Greyvalue differences of adjacent pixels have a prior probability distribution

$$ P(\Delta I = \Delta i) = \text{const} \cdot \exp\left(-\left|\frac{\Delta i}{\lambda}\right|^{\beta}\right) \qquad (2) $$

with $\beta = 0.5$ and $\lambda = \left(\frac{E\{|\Delta I|^{\beta}\}}{2}\right)^{1/\beta}$, where ΔI is a random variable for the difference between greyvalues (depending on the distance between the measured image points).

2. Greyvalue differences of pixels across an edge have a uniform distribution.
3. The visible shape of the model deviates from the projection of the model into the image plane by gaussian variability orthogonal to the projected model segments with a variance equal to the projection of σ into the image ($\sigma \in [0.1m, 0.5m]$).

While these assumptions sound reasonable, the algorithm contains in addition the following implicit assumptions:

4. All modelled edges are visible in the image as a a greyvalue *discontinuity*, because the model assumes that they affect only one greyvalue difference. Slow and gradual differences which commonly occur on aerodynamically shaped cars, however, affect more than one greyvalue difference.
5. Each line orthogonal to a projected model segment contains exactly one greyvalue discontinuity. In practice, this assumption can be violated by having zero discontinuities (for example if there is no vehicle-background-contrast) or more than one (in tapered model-segment configurations where model segments are close to each other).

In order to combine these assumptions, the algorithm selects points on the projected model segments, called *sample points* $\boldsymbol{\mu}_k \in \mathbb{R}^2 (k = 1..n)$ in this document. Subsequently, the algorithm looks for an image discontinuity on a line of points $\boldsymbol{\nu}_{k,j} = \boldsymbol{\mu}_k + j\, d\, \mathbf{r}_k$ ($j = -8..8, |\mathbf{r}_k| = 1$) orthogonal to the projected model segment. At each of these measure points $\boldsymbol{\nu}_{k,j}$, it computes the greyvalue difference

$$\Delta i(\boldsymbol{\nu}_{k,j}) = I(\boldsymbol{\mu}_k + (j+1/2)d\,\mathbf{r}_k) - I(\boldsymbol{\mu}_k + (j-1/2)d\,\mathbf{r}_k) \qquad (3)$$

using the image greyvalues $I(\cdot)$. The distance d between the measure points is chosen to be $\text{proj}(\sigma)/4$.

Then, the algorithm computes the probability of all greyvalues on the measure point line to be $P(\Delta \mathbf{i}_k) = \prod_{m=-8}^{8} f_L(\Delta i(\boldsymbol{\nu}_{k,m}))$. The conditional probability of this given that the object border (specified by the random variable $\mathbf{N}_k$) crosses near measure point $\boldsymbol{\nu}_{k,j}$ is given by

$$P(\Delta \mathbf{i}_k | \mathbf{N}_k = \boldsymbol{\nu}_{k,j}) = \prod_{m=-8}^{j-1} f_L(\Delta i(\boldsymbol{\nu}_{k,m})) \frac{1}{256} \prod_{m=j+1}^{8} f_L(\Delta i(\boldsymbol{\nu}_{k,m})) \qquad (4)$$

$$= \frac{P(\Delta \mathbf{i}_k)}{256\, f_L(\Delta i(\boldsymbol{\nu}_{k,j}))}. \qquad (5)$$

Assumption 3 expands to a prior distributing for the object border location

$$P(\mathbf{N}_k = \boldsymbol{\nu}_{k,j} | \boldsymbol{\mu}_k) = \text{const} \cdot \exp\left(-\frac{\|\boldsymbol{\nu}_{k,j} - \boldsymbol{\mu}_k\|^2}{2\text{proj}(\sigma)^2}\right) = \text{const} \cdot \exp\left(-\frac{|j|}{16}\right). \qquad (6)$$

Using these two formulas, the following figure-of-merit function is defined which has to be optimized:

$$l(\boldsymbol{\mu}) = \ln \frac{P(\Delta \mathbf{i}|\boldsymbol{\mu})}{P(\Delta \mathbf{i})} = \ln \prod_{k=1}^{n} \frac{P(\Delta \mathbf{i}_k|\boldsymbol{\mu}_k)}{P(\Delta \mathbf{i}_k)} \tag{7}$$

$$= \ln \prod_{k=1}^{n} \sum_{j=-8}^{8} \frac{P(\Delta \mathbf{i}_k|\boldsymbol{\nu}_{k,j}) \, P(\boldsymbol{\nu}_{k,j}|\boldsymbol{\mu}_k)}{P(\Delta \mathbf{i}_k)} \quad . \tag{8}$$

To perform the maximisation of this function, the Bayes formula is applied to combine (5) and (6) to a posterior probability for the border location:

$$P(\boldsymbol{\nu}_{k,h}|\Delta \mathbf{i}_k, \boldsymbol{\mu}_k) = \frac{P(\Delta \mathbf{i}_k|\boldsymbol{\nu}_{k,h}, \boldsymbol{\mu}_k) P(\boldsymbol{\nu}_{k,h}|\boldsymbol{\mu}_k)}{P(\Delta \mathbf{i}_k|\boldsymbol{\mu}_k)} \tag{9}$$

$$= \frac{P(\Delta \mathbf{i}_k|\boldsymbol{\nu}_{k,h}) P(\boldsymbol{\nu}_{k,h}|\boldsymbol{\mu}_k)}{\sum_{j=-l}^{l} P(\Delta \mathbf{i}_k|\boldsymbol{\nu}_{k,j}) P(\boldsymbol{\nu}_{k,j}|\boldsymbol{\mu}_k)} . \tag{10}$$

The expectation value of this distribution gives an estimator for the border location: $\hat{\boldsymbol{\nu}}_k = E\{\boldsymbol{\nu}_k|\Delta \mathbf{i}_k, \boldsymbol{\mu}_k\}$.

Finally, it can be shown that setting $\boldsymbol{\mu}$ to

$$\boldsymbol{\mu} = \min_{\boldsymbol{\mu}} \sum_{k=1}^{n} \|\hat{\boldsymbol{\nu}}_k - \boldsymbol{\mu}_k\|^2 \tag{11}$$

increases the figure-of-merit function $l(\boldsymbol{\mu})$ and the iterated execution of this approach eventually leads to a (possibly local) maximum. Therefore, it is possible not only to design a single figure-of-merit function measuring the overall quality of model fitting, but also to derive a greedy algorithm for finding its optimum. Furthermore, it is also possible to take $\hat{\boldsymbol{\nu}}_k$ as the measurement of a Kalman filter and $\boldsymbol{\mu}_k$ as the predicted measurement, which also results in equ. (11) to be minimized, just with a second additive term minimizing the squared distance between estimated and corrected vehicle state.

On the Relationship Between Image and Motion Segmentation

Adrian Barbu[1] and Song Chun Zhu[2]

[1] UCLA, Computer Science Department,
Los Angeles, CA 90095
abarbu@ucla.edu
http://www.cs.ucla.edu/~abarbu/Research/
[2] UCLA, Statistics Department,
Los angeles, CA 90095
sczhu@stat.ucla.edu
http://www.stat.ucla.edu/~sczhu/

Abstract. In this paper we present a generative model for image sequences, which can be applied to motion segmentation and tracking, and to image sequence compression. The model consists of regions of relatively constant color that have a motion model explaining their motion in time. At each frame, the model can allow accretion and deletion of pixels. We also present an algorithm for maximizing the posterior probability of the image sequence model, based on the recently introduced Swendsen-Wang Cuts algorithm. We show how one can use multiple cues and model switching in a reversible manner to make better bottom-up proposals. The algorithm works on the 3d spatiotemporal pixel volume to reassign entire trajectories of constant color in very few steps, while maintaining detailed balance.

1 Introduction

Motion segmentation and tracking can be performed together in a unified way as it was clearly showed in [3]. However, there is still a lot to be done in this direction. Better motion and shape priors should be studied, the 3d reconstruction of the moving objects and their motion should be used wherever possible as better motion models. Flexible motion models (2d or 3d) should also be studied.

Another important and very interesting open question is the relationship between the image segmentation and motion segmentation. When we see a moving scene, we perceive it as some "segmentation". But this is neither image segmentation based on image intensity, neither motion segmentation based on motion. Somehow, our brain is capable of combining all the existing information to give a better segmentation than either the intensity based or the motion based segmentation. How does the brain combine the two different segmentations cues into a single segmentation? In this paper, we try to give an answer to this question using generative models in a probabilistic Bayesian framework.

There are some classical examples that should be explained by a system combining image and motion segmentation. For example, if one has an image of

W.J. MacLean (Ed.): SCVMA 2004, LNCS 3667, pp. 51–63, 2006.

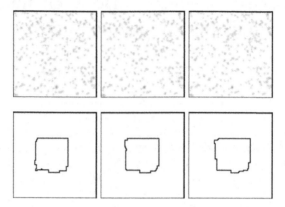

Fig. 1. A rectangle of uniform texture moving in a similar background is properly modeled and segmented by our method

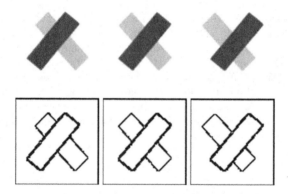

Fig. 2. Two slanted rectangles of constant intensity moving horizontally create false motion cues at their intersection points. Also, there is no motion information inside the rectangles. But they are properly modeled and segmented by our method.

uniform texture with an object of the exactly same texture moving in the center of the image, the system should be able to correctly segment the object out based on motion. Here the motion segmentation provides the clues for the desired "segmentation". On the other hand, in an image sequence with objects of constant intensity, the motion cues are very sparse, namely only at the boundary of the objects and in direction perpendicular to the boundary. Some corners could even have motion not compatible with any of the moving objects of the scene (see Fig. 2). The desired "segmentation" has to integrate these sparse and sometimes misleading motion cues and combine them with intensity information to obtain a good segmentation, based on the prior information that motion boundaries often occur at intensity boundaries. Here the image segmentation provides most of the cues for the desired "segmentation".

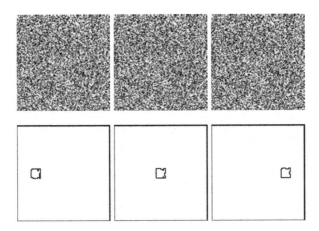

Fig. 3. A 10x10 square of random pixels moving in a similar background at a speed of 30 pixels per frame is properly modeled and segmented by our method

Our generative model can easily handle these examples, as one can see in Figures 1 and 2. Moreover, it can also handle extreme cases with large motion as shown in Figure 3. In a square of size 100x100 filled with random pixels, a 10x10 square of random pixels is moving, on three frames, with the speed of 30 pixels per frame. By having the right motion hypotheses, our framework can segment and track the little square.

It is our belief that image segmentation and motion segmentation should be performed together, in a hierarchical fashion. A reason for this is the fact that intensity regions can already have their motion inferred, so the motion segmentation of an object with many intensity regions can be thought as just combining the intensity regions based on their common motions.

In other words, the first level is a special kind of image segmentation into regions of relatively constant intensity moving by some motion model, then these regions are combined together, on a second level of representation and computation, based solely on their motion models to give the motion segmentation. See Figures 11 and 12 for motion segmentation results based on simple clustering of the motion models of the intensity regions.

However, there is more to the second level (of motion segmentation) than just clustering the motions of the intensity regions. The higher level model can be a 3d model (rigid 3d motion for example) while the motions of the different image regions would be usually much simpler (planar motion models). Together, the intensity regions can provide the necessary information to allow the computation of a global 3d model, even though each of them individually doesn't have that information. Also, the higher level will have priors for motion segmentation on top of the image segmentation priors of the lower level.

The purpose of this paper is to present the model and a computational framework for the first level, that of segmenting and tracking of regions of relatively constant intensity and motion. In a subsequent paper we will show how to integrate this level with the second level of motion segmentation tracked in time.

Our framework is based on a probabilistic Bayesian generative model that explains all the pixels in the motion sequence. Usually (see [2, 3, 7, 9]), probabilistic models for motion are put on the spatiotemporal gradient of the image, without explaining the original image sequence. This is based on the assumption that the scene is lambertian without any abrupt changes in intensity or motion. This highly restricts the applicability of the gradient based methods.

In our framework we use the gradient based motion models as one kind of bottom-up proposals. Since they do not always give the correct motion model, our algorithm will take them, and accept or reject them based on the Metropolis-Hastings algorithm and our posterior probability.

An important aspect of our framework is that we don't try to track pixels, we try to track small regions of relatively constant color. This allows the usage of motion models beyond the classical translational models.

This work was sponsored by the NSF SGER grant IIS-0240148.

2   The Image Sequence Model

Let $I = (I_0, ..., I_k)$ be the observed image sequence. We want to find a partition R of I into an unknown number n of subsets R_i of relatively constant color or texture, which we call region trajectories, or just regions. Each R_i represents the trajectory of a patch of constant color or uniform texture tracked in time by a rigid motion model (translation, affine, projective or homography). We denote by R_i^t the region R_i at frame t.

The model of R_i consists of an image model and a motion model. The image model models all pixels that are accreted (their projection through the motion model in the previous frame falls outside the region R_i). In our framework, we chose the image model to be a Gaussian model $\mathcal{N}(\mu_i, \sigma_i)$. The motion model T_i^t is a transformation that describes how the region changes from frame t to frame $t + 1$. At each frame it is a translation, affine, projective or homography transformation. Later on we could consider even flexible models. Since the reconstruction from the previous frame through the motion model is not perfect, we have a noise model η_i modeled by a Gaussian $\mathcal{N}(\nu_i, \tau_i)$. Thus

$$I_{t+1}(T_i^t(x)) - I_t(x) \sim \mathcal{N}(\nu_i, \tau_i), \ \forall x \in R_i^t \ s.t. \ T_i^t(x) \in R_i^{t+1} \qquad (1)$$

Let $T_i = \{T_i^t\}$ be all the transformations for region R_i and $T = \{T_1, ..., T_n\}$ be the transformations of all the regions. Similarly let $\theta = \{\theta_1, ..., \theta_n\}$ be the image models and $\eta = \{\eta_1, ..., \eta_n\}$ be the noise models for all the regions. For now, we assume the regions are independent. In a subsequent paper, we will group them into moving objects, based on their motion similarity.

Thus the hidden variables are:

$$W = \{n, (R_i, \theta_i, T_i, \eta_i), i \in \{1, .., n\}\} \qquad (2)$$

We work in a Bayesian framework with prior and likelihood:

$$P(W|I) \propto P(I|W)P(W) = P(I|R, \theta, T, \eta)p(R, \theta, T, \eta)$$

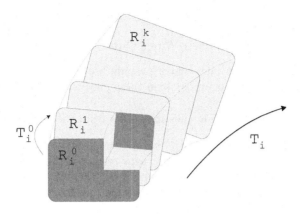

Fig. 4. A region trajectory R_i has an image model that explains the *accreted* pixels (shown in dark), whose projection in the previous frame is not inside R_i, and a motion model for the rest of the pixels (shown in light color)

We assume a Markov dependence of each frame on the previous one:

$$P(I|R,\theta,T,\eta) = \prod_t P(I_{t+1}|I_t,R,\theta,T,\eta)$$

The pixels $I^{t+1}(R_i)$ of region R_i at frame $t+1$ are reconstructed from I_t, R, θ, T, η as follows: All pixels $x \in R_i^{t+1}$ whose back-projection by T_i^t falls inside R_i^t are modeled by the noise model η_i. Let M_i^{t+1} be these pixels, namely:

$$M_i^{t+1} = \{x \in R_i^{t+1}, x = T_i^t(y), y \in R_i^t\} \tag{3}$$

The pixels of $R_i^{t+1} - M_i^{t+1}$ are modeled by the image model θ_i. Thus:

$$P(I_{t+1}|I_t,R,\theta,T,\eta) = \prod_i \prod_{x=T_i^t(y)\in M_i^{t+1}} P_{\eta_i}(I(x)-I(y)) \prod_i \prod_{x\in R_i^{t+1}-M_i^{t+1}} P_{\theta_i}(I(x))$$

$$\propto \prod_i e^{-\frac{1}{2\tau_i^2}\sum_{x=T_i^t(y)\in M_i^{t+1}}(I(x)-I(y)-\nu_i)^2} \prod_i e^{-\frac{1}{2\sigma_i^2}\sum_{x\in R_i^{t+1}-M_i^{t+1}}(I(x)-\mu_i)^2} \tag{4}$$

The prior is simplified as $P(R,\theta,T,\eta) = P(R|T)P(T)P(\theta)P(\eta)$. For now we take $P(T) = \prod_i \prod_t \delta(T_i^t - T_i^{t-1})$. We also assume $P(\theta)$ and $P(\eta)$ to be uniform.

The factor $P(R|T)$ represents that the regions should be big, should have a smooth boundary, and be consistent with the transformations T. We take:

$$P(R|T) \propto \prod_i \exp[-\alpha \mathrm{Vol}(R_i)^{0.9} - \beta \mathrm{Area}(\partial R_i) - \gamma(n_i^{in} + n_i^{out})] \tag{5}$$

where n_i^{in} represents the number of pixels of R_i whose back-projection to the previous frame is not in R_i, and n_i^{out} represents the number of pixels of R_i whose projection to the next frame is not in R_i.

3   Space-Time Segmentation by Swendsen-Wang Cuts

3.1   The Multi-cue Swendsen-Wang Cuts

Sometimes there are many cues which provide bottom-up information for the graph partitioning. How can we combine these cues while maintaining detailed balance?

Great help for answering this question comes from the following.

Theorem 1. *Let $q_1, ..., q_n$ be Markov moves with transition kernels $K_1, ..., K_n$, such that all q_i observe detailed balance with respect to the same probability p. Let $\alpha_1, ..., \alpha_n \geq 0$ be such that $\alpha_1 + ... + \alpha_n = 1$. Then the Markov move q that at each step randomly selects an $i \in \{1, ..., n\}$ with probability α_i and executes q_i has transition kernel:*

$$K = \sum_{i=1}^{n} \alpha_i K_i \qquad (6)$$

and also satisfies the detailed balance equation for p.

From this theorem, the answer to our question comes easily:

Corollary 2. *Let $SW_1, ..., SW_n$ be a number of Swendsen-Wang Cuts algorithms working on the same nodes V and same posterior probability P, with adjacency graphs $G_1, ..., G_n$. Let $\alpha_1, ..., \alpha_n \geq 0$ be fixed numbers such that $\alpha_1 + ... + \alpha_n = 1$. Then the move consisting of randomly choosing an i with probability α_i and executing SW_i is reversible and ergodic.*

We can think of each SW_i as a hypothesis that is being tested in a reversible manner.

The only restriction in using the above results is that the α_i be fixed. We can still use, if possible, bottom-up information to select good values for α_i, resulting in an efficient visiting schedule of the different SW_i as long as the schedule is fixed a priori. This way we can have some hypotheses more likely than other, so they are tested more often. For each hypothesis, the algorithm will be efficient at the places where that hypothesis is valid. By combining a good set of hypotheses, the algorithm will be efficient everywhere.

3.2   Multi-cue SW Cuts for Motion

The SW Cut algorithm is most efficient when the sampled connected components closely resemble the segments in the desired segmentation. Thus, in order to have good bottom-up information, the proposals should be long region trajectories. For that, the edges of the SW graph must be very informative. It is not enough just to have them on a 3d lattice with weights based on pixel similarity, we have to bring in the motion and intensity hypotheses.

A motion hypothesis is a k-tuple $\boldsymbol{m} = (T^1, ..., T^k)$ for the hypothesized affine transformation at each frame. Usually, we use only constant velocity hypotheses $(v, v, ..., v)$. In the future, we will use more complex hypotheses which are based on more complex motion (rotation, zoom, etc).

Fig. 5. The 2d space of x-motion (x-axis) and intensity (y-axis) of feature points from Figures 1,2,9,10 and 12 respectively. Darker means more instances of features.

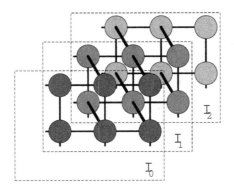

Fig. 6. For each hypothesis $(G, T^1, ..., T^k)$, the SW graph is a lattice at each frame (solid thin lines), and between frames $t - 1$ and t there are edges only in the direction $x \rightarrow T^t(x)$ (thick lines). Shown is the SW graph for hypothesis $(G, v, ..., v), v = (-1, 0)$.

An intensity hypothesis is an intensity model G (we use gaussian, but we can also use histograms of filter responses for texture, or a histogram of intensity values for the clutter model).

Together they compose a hypothesis $h = (G, m) = (G, T^1, ..., T^k)$.

To obtain motion hypotheses, we extract some feature points (corners) and we perform clustering in the joint space of intensity-motion hypotheses of the corners. We obtain a few (less than 20) clusters. For each such cluster we will have a SW graph. For illustration, we present in Figure 5 the x-motion (x-axis) and intensity (y-axis) obtained from the feature points of Figures 1,2,9,10 and 12 respectively.

For a hypothesis $(G, T^1, ..., T^k)$, the SW graph is a lattice at each frame, and from frame $t - 1$ to t consists only of edges $x \rightarrow T_t(x)$. This way the edges for each graph are in a reasonable number, while being able to cover the most likely motions.

For hypothesis $h = (G, T^1, ..., T^k)$ with $G = (\mu, \sigma^2)$, and x at frame t, define

$$g_h(x) = \frac{(I_t(x) - \mu)^2}{2\sigma^2}, d_h(x) = |I_t(x) - I_{t+1}(T^{t+1}(x))|, d^h(x) = |I_t(x) - I_{t-1}((T^t)^{-1}(x))| \tag{7}$$

$$q_h(x) = \begin{cases} d_h(x) & \text{if } x \in I_0 \\ d^h(x) & \text{if } x \in I_k \\ (d_h(x) + d^h(x))/2 & \text{else} \end{cases} \tag{8}$$

Then the edge weights for hypothesis $h = (G, T^1, ..., T^k)$ are:

$$q(x, y) = e^{-0.1(g_h(x)+g_h(y)+q_h(x)+q_h(y))} \qquad (9)$$

To get connected components, we use the Wolff variant, which grows a connected component from a seed. First we sample a hypothesis $h = (G, \mathbf{m})$ proportional to the sum of the saliencies $S_h(x)$ of all pixels x. Then the seed s is sampled from a "cry map" C_h of how well each pixel fits its assigned image model and motion model. Small value $C_h(x)$ means x fits well its assigned model or is not salient to this h. We take $C_h(x) = \alpha S_h(x)(g_m + q_m(x))$, with g_m, q_m from (7),(8), m being the current model of x and α is chosen so that $\sum_x C_h(x) = 1$. Then, by sampling the seed s from the pmf C_h, we usually obtain a pixel that is unhappy with its current model and salient to the current h. Then we use the SW graph G_h corresponding to h to grow the seed s to a component C, and flip its label. It is easy to check that

Theorem 3. *(SW Cuts with "cry map"). Consider a candidate component C selected by SWC using a "cry map" C_h^A (for state A), as described above. Let $q_c(C|A) = \sum_{x \in C} C_h^A(x)$. If the proposed move to reassign C from G_l to $G_{l'}$ is accepted with probability*

$$\alpha(A \to B) = \min(1, \frac{q_c(C|B)}{q_c(C|A)} \frac{\prod\limits_{e \in C(C, V_{l'} - C)} (1 - q_e)}{\prod\limits_{e \in C(C, V_l - C)} (1 - q_e)} \frac{q(l|C, B, G_h)}{q(l'|C, A, G_h)} \frac{p(B|I)}{p(A|I)}) \qquad (10)$$

then the Markov chain is reversible and ergodic.

Thus basically we have an SW move for each hypothesis h, which is reversible. Then the overall move is also reversible by Corollary 2.

The two extreme cases presented in the introduction, can explain very well what happens. In the case of the rectangle of same texture as the background, the chosen component C_{seed} are relatively small, but the motion information is very peaked, so the correct motion is sampled most of the time. Thus the components that are flipped are long "fibers", relatively thin, as shown in Figure 7.

Fig. 7. For an image sequence like Fig. 1 but with more texture, we present samples from the graph in the direction of motion hypotheses $(0,0)$ and $(4,0)$ respectively. We see that for the right hypothesis, the SW reassigns long fibers.

Fig. 8. For the image in Fig. 2, we present samples from the graph in the direction of hypothesis of motion $(0,0)$. For clarity, the component of the background has been removed. Even though the motion hypothesis is not correct for the moving rectangles, the samples are big and meaningful in both space and time.

In the case of the two slanted rectangles of uniform color, the lattice edges at each time frame have big weight, so the chosen component C_{seed} is big, and even though the motion information might not be precise, the sampled component C will be big in both space and time, as shown in Figure 8. In this case, the problem is more of a "blob" tracking problem.

For real world problems, the components sampled will be between the extreme cases, making use of the available intensity or motion information.

3.3   Model Switching in Swendsen-Wang Cuts

It is clear that in our approach, the motion models are very important. If, at each step, the proposed image models are inappropriate, the move will be rejected and the algorithm will slow down drastically. This is why we have to combine the model switching with the Swendsen-Wang Cuts reassignment in a single step:

Theorem 4. *(SW Cuts with model switching). In the notations of [1], consider a candidate component V_0 selected by SWC. Let $q_m(\mu_i|V_i)$ be a proposal probability from which the model μ_i of a subgraph V_i of the partition is chosen by sampling. If the proposed move to reassign V_0 from G_l to $G_{l'}$, and then change the model of G_l from μ_l^A to μ_l^B and the model of $G_{l'}$ from $\mu_{l'}^A$ to $\mu_{l'}^B$ is accepted with probability*

$$\alpha(A \to B) = \min(1, \frac{q_m(\mu_l^A|V_l \cup V_0)q_m(\mu_{l'}^A|V_{l'} - V_0)}{q_m(\mu_l^B|V_l - V_0)q_m(\mu_{l'}^B|V_{l'} \cup V_0)} \frac{\prod_{e \in C(V_0,V_{l'} - V_0)}(1 - q_e)}{\prod_{e \in C(V_0,V_l - V_0)}(1 - q_e)} \frac{q(l|V_0, B, G_o)p(B|I)}{q(l'|V_0, A, G_o)p(A|I)})$$

$$(11)$$

then the Markov chain is reversible and ergodic.

For the model proposal probabilities, we will have three kind of proposals $q_1(T_i|I)$, $q_2(T_i|I), q_3(T_i|I)$ used with frequency $0.98, 0.01, 0.01$ respectively. Each proposal is one type of reversible SW move and since we are using them with constant frequency, the overall move is still reversible. First proposal, is $q_1(T_i|I) = \delta(T_i)$ enforces no change in model. Second proposal is $q_2(T_i|I) = c$ is uniform in a discrete window of possible motions. This ensures that even if all other proposals fail, one could still obtain the right model after enough time. The third proposal is the constant velocity affine model from [3]. The usefulness of the Cremers model (working on the spatiotemporal gradient $\nabla_3 I = (I_x, I_y, I_t)$) for our purpose is that it can be computed incrementally, so we always have it available for all regions, without much overhead. It is,

$$q_3(T_i|I) \propto \prod_{(x,y)\in R_i} \exp\left(-\frac{p_i^T M(x,y)^T \nabla_3 I}{|p_i|^2 |M(x,y)^T \nabla_3 I|^2}\right) \tag{12}$$

where

$$T_i^t = \begin{pmatrix} a_i & b_i & c_i \\ d_i & e_i & f_i \\ 0 & 0 & 1 \end{pmatrix}, p_i = (a_i, b_i, c_i, d_i, e_i, f_i, 1)^T, M(x,y) = \begin{pmatrix} x & y & 1 & 0 & 0 & 0 & 0 \\ 0 & 0 & 0 & x & y & 1 & 0 \\ 0 & 0 & 0 & 0 & 0 & 0 & 1 \end{pmatrix}$$

and $\nabla_3 I = (I_x, I_y, I_t)$ is the spatiotemporal gradient of the image sequence I. This corresponds to a velocity field at frame t: $v_i(x,t) = T_i^t \begin{pmatrix} x \\ y \\ 1 \end{pmatrix} = M(x,y)p_i$.

Since we discretized our model parameter space, we can easily compute the proposal probability at each bin and then sample from the discretized proposal probability $q(p_i)$, without having to compute the eigenvalues and eigenvectors.

4 Experiments

We have already presented some experiments on synthetic sequences in Figures 1,2,3. Our experiments are performed on 3-5 frames of grayscale image sequences.

Other results are presented in Figures 9,10, 11 and 12. We see that the framework is capable of producing new image regions when new objects are visible

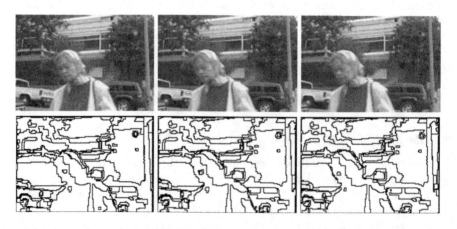

Fig. 9. A moving person in front of a moving background

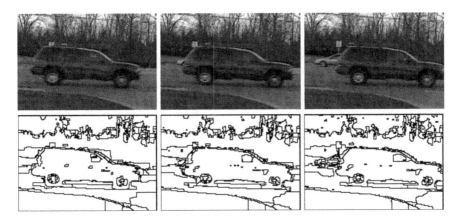

Fig. 10. A car appears from behind another car in a static background

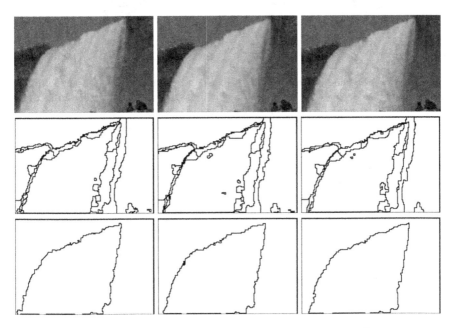

Fig. 11. Waterfall with a moving background. Input sequence (first row),image segmentation (second row) and motion segmentation obtained by clustering of the velocities of the regions (third row).

in the image, like the small car in Figure 10. In figures 11 and 12, we also show some motion segmentation results obtained by simple clustering on the motion velocities of the regions. The motion segmentations can be improved by having priors on the motion regions, and not assuming the regions to be independent. Animated demos for all examples can be found on the web at http://www.cs.ucla.edu/~abarbu/Research/SWMotion3d/ .

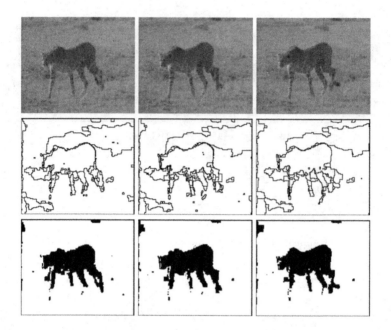

Fig. 12. A walking cheetah on a moving background. Input sequence (first row),image segmentation (second row) and motion segmentation obtained by clustering of the velocities of the regions (third row).

5   Limitations and Future Work

Currently, the computation time is quite high, between 2 and 10 minutes per frame for a 100x100 image on a PC. One reason is that the graph edges are still not informative enough. For example, if one has two neighboring regions of very similar intensity and no texture, moving differently, the edges will be strong and the algorithm will not be able to separate the regions quickly. We will examine how to use belief propagation and top-down information to change the edges of the graph to be more informative. Also, better shape priors which can be quickly computed are needed to be studied.

References

1. Barbu A., Zhu S.C.: Graph Partition by Swendsen-Wang Cuts IEEE International Conference in Computer Vision (2003)
2. Black M. J., Jepson A. D.: Estimating optical flow in segmented images using variable order parametric models with local deformations. IEEE Trans PAMI **18** no. 10 (1996) 972–986
3. Cremers D., Soatto S.: Variational Space-Time Motion Segmentation, ICCV, (2003)
4. Horn, B.K.P.: Robot Vision. MIT Press. Cambridge, Ma. (1986)
5. Gaucher, L. and Medioni, G. Accurate Motion Flow with Discontinuities. ICCV, pp 695-702. 1999.

6. Torr P.H.S.: Geometric motion segmentation and model selection. Philosophical Trans of the Royal Society A, (1998) 1321–1340

7. Weiss Y.: Smoothness in Layers: Motion segmentation using nonparametric mixture estimation. Proc. of IEEE CVPR (1997) 520-527

8. Wolff U., "Collective Monte Carlo updating for spin systems", *Phys. Rev. Lett.*, vol. 62, no. 4, pp. 361-364, 1989.

9. Yuille A.L., Grzywacz N.M.: A mathematical analysis of the motion coherence theory. Int. J. Computer Vision **3** (1989) 155–175

Motion Detection Using Wavelet Analysis and Hierarchical Markov Models

Cédric Demonceaux[1,2] and Djemâa Kachi-Akkouche[1]

[1] C.R.E.A, E.A. 3299,
7, rue du moulin neuf, 80000 Amiens, France
[2] L.A.M.F.A., UMR 6140,
33, rue Saint-Leu, 80000 Amiens, France
{cedric.demonceaux, djemaa.kachi}@u-picardie.fr

Abstract. This paper deals with the motion detection problem. This issue is of key importance in many application fields. To solve this problem, we compute the dominant motion in the sequence using a wavelet analysis and robust techniques. So, we obtain an estimation of the dominant motion on several image resolutions. This method permits to define a hierarchical Markov model in a natural way. Thanks to this modelization, we overcome two problems: the solution sensibility in relation to the initial condition with a Markov random field, and the temporal aliasing. Moreover, we obtain a semi-iterative algorithm faster than using the multi-scale techniques. Thus, we introduce a fast and robust algorithm in order to compute the motion detection in an image sequence. This method is validated on real image sequences.

1 Introduction and Previous Works

Motion detection is an important problem in many applications: obstacle detection, video coding, content-based retrieval, video surveillance... Motion detection consists in separating the image in two regions : stationary region relatively with the camera motion and moving region. With a fixed camera, a difference between two consecutive images can be sufficient to get a bi-partition of the picture in a stationary zone and a motion zone. However, this type of method is very sensitive to the change of illumination conditions. Many authors have proposed an improvement of this method. Several methods use statical tests such as Hsu and al [9] who assume the intensity locally affine, Rosin [17] who modelizes the noise in the sequence by a normal distribution. Aach and al [1], Sifakis [18] define the inter-frame difference with a probability density function. Another approach consists in regularizing the masks of motion detection by a Markov model [4], [11].

With a mobile camera, the problem is more difficult. We can use some constraints on the apparent displacement field of the camera supposed known [19]. Another way consists to compensate the sequence with the dominant motion. It allows to return to the simpler case of a fixed camera. Then, classical technics of

W.J. MacLean (Ed.): SCVMA 2004, LNCS 3667, pp. 64–75, 2006.

thresholding [10], or bayesian methods [14], [15] are used. An initial spatial partition based on intensity, texture or color information can be used too [13]. Moreover, some techniques compute simultaneously motion and detection [5], [6].

In many methods, the motion computation in the image is performed by the measure of the displaced frame difference $(DFD(x,t) = I(x+v,t+1) - I(x,t))$. Indeed, this method is often preferred to the differential method because it allows to estimate great displacements in image sequence $I(x,t)$. But, as the DFD is not linear, the motion estimation by DFD is computed by gradient descent. This method is more expensive in computing times than the proposed approach in this work. In this article, we estimate the motion in the sequence from the Brightness Change Constraint Equation (B.C.C.E.). The problem of the great displacement estimation, i.e the aliasing problem, is overcomed thanks to a wavelet analysis of this equation and a motion compensation between each scale. This method enables to obtain a motion estimation at each scale by the resolution of an over-determined linear system. The study of B.C.C.E at each scale gives a measurement characterizing the conformity with the dominant motion for each point. To solve the motion detection problem from the obtained multi-scale data, we suggest to modelize the problem by a hierarchical markovian model. This model combines an a priori dependence in space and in scale with a Markov random field on the coarsest level of the image. Chardin [16], who used these fields to texture segmentation, established that these models are in fact a generalization of the multi-scale approach of [7] and permit to obtain better results in shorter cpu time. Moreover, contrary to the multi-scale approach which only uses observations at the finer scale, the hierarchical definition of the problem uses observations at each scale of the image. This allows to overcome the temporal aliasing problem generated by the motion estimation with differential methods. Thanks to the wavelet analysis and to the hierarchical modelization, the method presented here is a fast method to detect moving objects in an image sequence.

This paper is organized as follows: In a first part, we compute the dominant motion in the scene by a wavelet analysis of the Brightness Change Constraint Equation and a robust M-estimator. This study enables us to obtain a fast estimation of the dominant motion at each resolution of the image. Then, in a second part, thanks to a hierarchical model, we see how to overcome the temporal aliasing problem inherent to the optical flow estimation by the differential method and how to solve the problem of motion detection. Finally, we see results on synthetic and real sequences.

2   Robust Dominant Motion Estimation

Let us consider image sequence $I((x,y),t)$. The problem is to estimate dominant motion $\vec{v}((x,y),t)$. To do that, we assume that the intensity constant in time for each physical point. Thus, by derivation, we obtain the well known Brightness Change Constraint Equation (B.C.C.E.):

$$\vec{\nabla}I((x,y),t).\vec{v}((x,y),t) + \frac{\partial I((x,y),t)}{\partial t} = 0 \qquad (1)$$

To estimate the dominant motion in the sequence, we solve the B.C.C.E. (1) by a wavelet analysis and an M-robust estimator.

Let us consider the wavelets basis $(\Psi^n)_{i=1\cdots N}$ in $L^2(\mathbf{R}^2)$ centered around the origin $(0,0)$, and let us consider the N functions centered around point $(2^j k_1, 2^j k_2)$ defined as :

$$\psi_{jk}^n(x,y) = 2^{-j}\psi^n(2^{-j}x - k_1, 2^{-j}y - k_2),$$

where $k = (k_1, k_2)$ and j is the index of resolution. Taking the inner product of (1) with Ψ_{jk}^n, we obtain the following system :

$$\langle \vec{\nabla} I.\vec{v} + \frac{\partial I}{\partial t}, \Psi_{jk}^n \rangle = 0 \qquad \forall n = 1 \cdots N, \tag{2}$$

where

$$\langle f, g \rangle = \int \int f(x)\overline{g(x)}dxdy.$$

We assume that dominant motion due to the camera movement $\vec{v}$ is affine, i.e:

$$\vec{v}(x,y) = B.\Theta^j, \quad (x,y) = (2^j k_1, 2^j k_2) \tag{3}$$

with

$$B = \begin{bmatrix} x & y & 1 & 0 & 0 & 0 \\ 0 & 0 & 0 & x & y & 1 \end{bmatrix}$$
$$\Theta^j = \left(a^j, b^j, c^j, d^j, e^j, f^j\right)^T$$

This model is a good tradeoff between complexity and representativeness. It can take into account many kinds of camera motion (translation, rotation, scaling, deformation).

By substituting affine model (3) in (2), we obtain for each j resolution the following system :

$$\forall n = 1..N, \forall (x,y) = (2^j k_1, 2^j k_2)$$
$$a^j \langle x\frac{\partial I}{\partial x}, \Psi_{jk}^n \rangle + b^j \langle y\frac{\partial I}{\partial x}, \Psi_{jk}^n \rangle + c^j \langle \frac{\partial I}{\partial x}, \Psi_{jk}^n \rangle +$$
$$d^j \langle x\frac{\partial I}{\partial y}, \Psi_{jk}^n \rangle + e^j \langle y\frac{\partial I}{\partial y}, \Psi_{jk}^n \rangle + f^j \langle \frac{\partial I}{\partial y}, \Psi_{jk}^n \rangle + \tag{4}$$
$$\langle \frac{\partial I}{\partial t}, \Psi_{jk}^n \rangle = 0$$

and by integrating by parts:

$$\forall (x,y) = (2^j k_1, 2^j k_2), \forall n = 1..N$$
$$a^j \left[\langle xI, \frac{\partial \Psi_{jk}^n}{\partial x} \rangle + \langle I, \Psi_{jk}^n \rangle \right] + b^j \langle yI, \frac{\partial \Psi_{jk}^n}{\partial x} \rangle + c^j \langle I, \frac{\partial \Psi_{jk}^n}{\partial x} \rangle +$$
$$d^j \langle xI, \frac{\partial \Psi_{jk}^n}{\partial y} \rangle + e^j \left[\langle yI, \frac{\partial \Psi_{jk}^n}{\partial y} \rangle + \langle I, \Psi_{jk}^n \rangle \right] + f^j \langle I, \frac{\partial \Psi_{jk}^n}{\partial y} \rangle = \tag{5}$$
$$\langle \frac{\partial I}{\partial t}, \Psi_{jk}^n \rangle$$

We obtain an over-determined system, $N \times 2^{p+q-2j}$ equations for an image of size $2^p \times 2^q$ and 6 unknowns at each j resolution. To avoid taking into account the points where hypothesis (3) is not valid, we solve system (5) by a robust M-estimator of Tukey's biweight [8].

2.1   Robust Motion Estimation

We note system (5):

$$M^j \Theta^j = P^j. \tag{6}$$

where M^j and P^j are respectively of dimension $6 \times 2^{p+q-2j} N$ and $1 \times 2^{p+q-2j} N$.

We solve this system (6) by a robust M-estimator of Tukey's biweight ρ. i.e. we look for Θ^j solution of:

$$\widehat{\Theta}^j = \arg\min_{\Theta} \sum_i \rho(r_i, C)$$
$$r_i = M^j \Theta^j(i) - P^j(i). \tag{7}$$

Solution $\widehat{\Theta}^j$ of (7) is computed by an Iteratively Reweighted Least Squares (IRLS):

$$\widehat{\Theta}^j = \min_{\Theta} \sum_{i=1}^{N \times 2^{p+q-2j}} w_i r_i^2, \tag{8}$$

where $w_i = \frac{1}{r_i}\frac{\partial\rho}{\partial x}(r_i)$. The resolution of (6) by a robust M-estimator allows us to avoid the outliers points i.e. the points which are not valid for assumption (3). Equation (8) gives an estimation of the motion at each j scale. However, in order to overcome the aliasing problem, we have to do motion compensation between each scale.

2.2   Motion Compensation

Considering the image sequence is sampled in time, we have to estimate the temporal derivative of I with a finite difference formula:

$$\langle \frac{\partial I}{\partial t}, \Psi^n_{jk} \rangle \simeq \langle I(t+1) - I(t), \Psi^n_{jk} \rangle$$

[2] proves that this approximation is valid if the optical flow verifies :

$$||\vec{v}|| < \text{K.size of wavelets support},$$

where K is a constant. So, dealing with a fine scale, only minor displacements can be estimated. Consequently, to compute large displacements, we have to compute recursively an estimation of the flow at a coarse scale and estimate the residual between this value and the real flow at a finer scale.

Let us suppose that at coarsest scale $j = J$, the solution of (6) is Θ^J. At scale $J - 1$, we can split vector Θ^J as follows :

$$\Theta^{J-1} = \mathcal{P}_{J \rightarrow J-1}(\Theta^J) + \epsilon^{J-1},$$

where $\mathcal{P}_{j \rightarrow j'}$ is the projector from scale j to scale j':

$$\mathcal{P}_{j \rightarrow j'}(\Theta) = diag(1 \quad 1 \quad 2^{j-j'} \quad 1 \quad 1 \quad 2^{j-j'}).\Theta$$

Let us introduce $\widetilde{I}_{\Theta^{J-1}}(t+1)$ as

$$\widetilde{I}_{\Theta^{J-1}}((x,y),t+1) = I((x,y) + \overrightarrow{V}_{\mathcal{P}_{J\to J-1}(\Theta^J)}, t+1).$$

The motion between $I(x,t)$ and $\widetilde{I}_{\Theta^J}(x,t+1)$ is exactly $\overrightarrow{V}_{\epsilon^{J-1}}$.

ϵ_p^{J-1} is the solution of system (6) where we replace $\langle \frac{\partial I}{\partial t}, \Psi_{(J-1)k}^n \rangle$ by $\langle \widetilde{I}_{\Theta_p^{J-1}}$ $(t+1) - I(t), \Psi_{(J-1)k}^n \rangle$.

Then, we compute iteratively the optical flow by motion compensation from the coarsest scale to the finest scale.

Thus, we obtain an estimation of the dominant motion at each j resolution.

3   Moving Objects Detection with Hierarchical Model

We have performed the dominant motion by a multi-scale method. This computation allows us to define in a natural way a hierarchical Markov model in all the resolutions of the image in order to solve moving object detection. This modelization has two advantages: it overcomes the problem of the sensibility to the initial conditions that we meet with a classical Iterated Conditional Modes [3] (I.C.M.), and it can solve the aliasing problem by compensation contrary to multi-scale methods such as [7], which only uses observations at the finer scale.

Let us note $S = \cup_{n=0}^J S^n$ where S^i indicates the level i of the image resolution, $E = \{E_s, s \in S\}$ and $Y = \{Y_s, s \in S\}$ respectively the random field of the labels of the detected motion and the random field of the observations. E_s can take two values, 0 or 1, where 1 corresponds to a site that does not conform with the dominant motion and 0 to a site that conforms with this motion. Let us note E^n the whole of the labels at level n, i.e. $E^n = \{E_s, s \in S^n\}$ and in the same way $Y^n = \{Y_s, s \in S^n\}$. Finally, let us note $\bar{i}$ the parent of site i, $\underline{i}$ the whole of the children of i and $\underline{i}$ the whole of the sites forming the tree of root i (fig 1). With this graphical structure and with some hypotheses described in [16], the distribution of (X, Y) can be written as :

$$P(E = e, Y = y) \propto exp - [\sum_{<i,j> \in S^J} v_{i,j}(e_i, e_j) \\ + \sum_{i \notin S^J} w_i(e_i, e_{\bar{i}}) + \sum_{i \in S} o_i(e_i, y_i)] \tag{9}$$

where $< i, j >$ designates pairs of neighbors in S^J, $v_{i,j}$ and w_i are local functions capturing respectively the spatial a priori and the hierarchical a priori, and o_i expresses the point-wise relation between observed variable y_i and unknown x_i. The associated MAP estimator to this distribution :

$$\hat{e} \in argmax_e P(e|y) = argmax_e P(e, y) \tag{10}$$

is computed from the following fast semi-iterative algorithm [16].

For the space and hierarchical potentials, we choose a priori usual functions of Potts type :

$$v_{i,j}(e_i, e_j) = \alpha[1 - \delta(e_i, e_j)],$$

$$w_i(e_i, e_{\bar{i}}) = \beta[1 - \delta(e_i, e_{\bar{j}})].$$

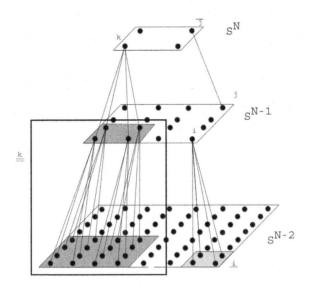

Fig. 1. Hierarchical structures. $\bar{j}$ the parent of the site j, $\underline{i}$ the whole of the children of i and $\underline{\underline{k}}$ the whole of the sites forming the tree of root k.

These potential functions enforce the homogenization of the labels field in space and in scale.

Let us define observations o_i which express the point-wise relation between observed variables y_i.

To assess the error of the motion estimation at point $(2^j k_1, 2^j k_2)$ we set at a j fixed scale :

$$E(j, k, \Theta^j) = \frac{\sum_{n=1}^{N} ||\langle \overrightarrow{\nabla} I, \Psi_{jk}^n \rangle || C}{\sum_{n=1}^{N} ||\langle \overrightarrow{\nabla} I, \Psi_{jk}^n \rangle ||^2} \tag{11}$$

$$\text{where } C = |\langle \overrightarrow{\nabla} I. \overrightarrow{V}_{\epsilon^j} + \tilde{I}_{\Theta^j}(t+1) - I(t), \Psi_{jk}^n \rangle|.$$

This measurement features an interesting property. Indeed, we can establish that

$$\forall \epsilon > 0,$$
$$E(j, k, \Theta^j) \leq \frac{\lambda_1}{\lambda_1 + \lambda_2} \epsilon \Rightarrow ||\overrightarrow{V}_{\epsilon^j} - \overrightarrow{V}_{jk}|| \leq \epsilon, \tag{12}$$
$$E(j, k, \Theta^j) \geq \sqrt{\frac{\lambda_2}{\lambda_1 + \lambda_2}} \epsilon \Rightarrow ||\overrightarrow{V}_{\epsilon^j} - \overrightarrow{V}_{jk}|| \geq \epsilon,$$

where $\overrightarrow{V}_{jk}$ is the real flow at scale j between images $I(t)$ and $\tilde{I}_{\Theta^j}(t+1)$ at point $(2^j k_1, 2^j k_2)$ and where λ_1, λ_2 are respectively the smallest and the greatest eigenvalue of

$$A = \sum_{n=1}^{N} \begin{pmatrix} |\langle I, \frac{\partial \Psi_{jk}^n}{\partial x} \rangle|^2 & \langle I, \frac{\partial \Psi_{jk}^n}{\partial x} \rangle \overline{\langle I, \frac{\partial \Psi_{jk}^n}{\partial y} \rangle} \\ \langle I, \frac{\partial \Psi_{jk}^n}{\partial x} \rangle \langle I, \frac{\partial \Psi_{jk}^n}{\partial y} \rangle & |\langle I, \frac{\partial \Psi_{jk}^n}{\partial y} \rangle|^2 \end{pmatrix}$$

We define $\forall \epsilon > 0$ the numbers

$$l_{jk} = \frac{\lambda_1}{\lambda_1 + \lambda_2}.\epsilon \text{ and } L_{jk} = \sqrt{\frac{\lambda_2}{\lambda_1 + \lambda_2}}.\epsilon. \tag{13}$$

According to (18), $E(j, k, \Theta^j)$ translates the error made by approximating the real optical flow at point $(2^j k_1, 2^j k_2)$ by V_{e^j} (velocity between the image $I(t)$ and the image $\widetilde{I}_{\Theta^j}(t+1)$).

If $E(j, k, \Theta^j) \leq l_{jk}$, we can assert that the error is smaller than ϵ and if $E(j, k, \Theta^j) \geq L_{jk}$, the error is larger than ϵ. This error will enable us to decide if point $(2^j k_1, 2^j k_2)$ follows the dominant motion up to ϵ.

Thanks to this measurement error, we define o_i as follows:

$$\forall x_i = (2^j k_1, 2^j k_2) \in S^j$$
$$o_i(e_i, y_i) = \begin{cases} f(E(j, k, \Theta^j_{e_i}), l_{jk}) & \text{if } e_i = 0 \\ 1 - f(E(j, k, \Theta^j_{e_i}), L_{jk}) & \text{if } e_i = 1 \end{cases} \qquad (14)$$

where

$$f(x, d) = \frac{1}{1 + e^{(\frac{-4}{d}(x-d))}}.$$

These potential functions enforce the sites to take label 0 (conform to motion) in the case where $E(j, k, \Theta^j_D) \leq l_{jk}$ and to take label 1 (not conform to motion) if $E(j, k, \Theta^j_D) \geq L_{jk}$.

So, we have defined a hierarchical Markov model in order to obtain a fast algorithm for the motion detection problem as we can see in the following section.

4 Experimental Results

The proposed method has been tested on many sequences. We here present results obtained on four sequences of size 256×256. In the results, the black areas represent the areas true to the dominant motion.

Synthetic sequence: This sequence is a synthetic sequence created to check that the motion compensation permits to detect the moving objects with large displacements. It is composed of a mobile bottom in translation of 13 pixels towards the left between the two images, of a circle in translation towards the right of 20 pixels and of a circle in translation to the bottom of 10 pixels (fig 3(b)). We estimated the dominant motion over 6 levels of resolution (fig 3(c)). Figure (2) shows the cpu times in seconds of various methods (on a PC Pentium III 933 Mhz). The results show the method allows to estimate large displacements in the scene thanks to the motion compensation between each scale of resolution. The moving object detection based on a hierarchical model is compared with two different resolutions (J=2 and J=3). Moreover, we compare these results with a traditional mono-resolution I.C.M. algorithm and without motion compensation (fig 3(f)). The modelization of the moving object detection problem by a hierarchical model gives good results. The results are almost similar except for the detection of two small zones in case J=2, normally in conformity with the dominant motion due to the temporal aliasing. A simple I.C.M. algorithm does not allow to detect correctly moving objects because of its sensitivity to initialization and of aliasing temporal and is moreover much longer than our method. In a general way, on the whole of the sequence, the modelization of problem on 3 levels of resolution gives good results.

	cpu times
Dominant motion estimation	1,8s
Motion Detection with J=3	1,2s
Motion Detection with J=2	2,9s
I.C.M mono resolution without motion compensation	10,8s

Fig. 2. cpu times for different methods

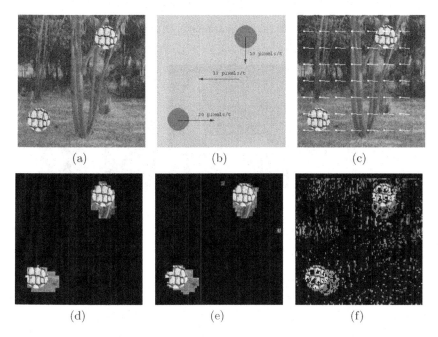

Fig. 3. $\epsilon = 1.2$, $\alpha = 0.4$, $\beta = 10$, (a) image test, (b) real motion, (c) dominant motion estimation, (d) motion detection with J=3, (e) J = 2 , (f) I.C.M. algorithm monoresolution without motion compensation

Fig. 4. $\epsilon = 1$, $\alpha = 0.4$, $\beta = 10$, (a) original image, (b) motion detection with J=3

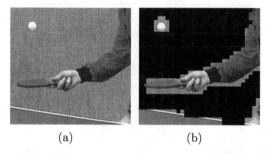

(a)   (b)

Fig. 5. $\epsilon = 1$, $\alpha = 0.4$, $\beta = 10$, (a) original image, (b) motion detection with J=4

(a)   (b)   (c)

Fig. 6. $\alpha = 5$, $\beta = 100$, (a) original image, (b) motion detection with J=3, $\epsilon = 1$, (c) motion detection with J=3, $\epsilon = 2$

Traffic sequence: In the sequence, the camera is motionless (fig 4(a)), 9 vehicles turn left and a vehicle in the top right advances towards the left. We detect correctly the vehicles, except the black car where the spatial gradient is too small to detect a motion.

Ping Pong sequence: The Ping-pong sequence has a Nil dominant motion (fig 5(a)). The arm of the player, his left hand, the ball and the racket are mobile and correctly detected.

Car sequence: The car sequence has a dominant motion from the right to the left caused by the camera displacement. Two cars move with independent motions and we can see a minor motion of the foliage due by the wind (fig 6(a)). We have tested our method with two different ϵ. With $\epsilon = 2$, as the foliage moves with minor motion, only the two cars are detected. Besides, with $\epsilon = 1$ a part of the tree is detected too.

5   Conclusion

We have introduced a new method of motion detection in an image sequence. This method estimates the dominant motion in the scene thanks to a wavelet analysis. This analysis enables us to obtain an estimation of the dominant motion at various scales by motion compensation. From these various data, we have defined a Markovian hierarchical model. Thanks to the fast algorithm of wavelets decomposition of Mallat [12], and to this hierarchical modelization, the method presented here is a fast method to detect moving objects in a sequence.

However, as we can see in the results, the hierarchical modelization generates blocks effects inherent to the structure. It would be interesting to add new interactions between the levels. Moreover, we will modelize the problem using a temporal data. So, we will use the label field previously estimated $(t - 1)$ to compute the next label field (t). This method will make it possible to avoid the detection of outliers due to the noise in sequences and to the motion estimation errors.

References

1. T. Aach, L. Duembgen, R. Mester, and D. Toth. Bayesian illumination-invariant motion detection. In *ICIP01*, pages 640–643, 2001.
2. C. Bernard. Discrete wavelet analysis: A new framework for fast optic flow computation. In *ECCV98*, pages 354–368, 1998.
3. J. Besag. On the statistical analysis of dirty pictures. *RoyalStat*, B-48(3):259–302, 1986.
4. P. Bouthemy and P. Lalande. Detection and tracking of moving objects based on a statistical regularization method in space and time. In *ECCV90*, pages 307–311, 1990.
5. M.M. Chang, A.M. Tekalp, and M.I. Sezan. Simultaneous motion estimation and segmentation. *IP*, 6(9):1326–1333, September 1997.
6. D. Cremers. A variational framework for image segmentation combining motion estimation and shape regularization. In *CVPR*, pages 53–58, 2003.
7. F. Heitz, P. Perez, and P. Bouthemy. Multiscale minimization of global energy functions in some visual recovery problems. *CVGIP*, 59(1):125–134, January 1994.
8. P.W. Holland and R.E. WelschHsu. Robust regression using iteratively reweighted least-squares. *Commun. Statist.-Theor. Meth.*, A6:813–827, 1977.
9. Y.Z. Hsu, H.H. Nagel, and G. Rekers. New likelihood test methods for change detection in image sequences. *CVGIP*, 26(1):73–106, April 1984.
10. M. Irani, B. Rousso, and S. Peleg. Detecting and tracking multiple moving objects using temporal integration. In *ECCV92*, pages 282–287, 1992.
11. F. Luthon, A. Caplier, and M. Lievin. Spatiotemporal mrf approach to video segmentation: Application to motion detection and lip segmentation. *SP*, 76(1):61–80, July 1999.
12. S.G. Mallat. A theory for multiresolution signal decomposition: The wavelet representation. *PAMI*, 11(7):674–693, July 1989.
13. H.T. Nguyen, M. Worring, and A. Dev. Detection of moving objects in video using a robust motion similarity measure. *IEEE Trans. on Image Processing*, 9(1):137–141, January 2000.
14. J.M. Odobez and P. Bouthemy. Detection of multiple moving objects using multiscale markov random fields, with camera compensation. In *ICIP94*, pages 257–261, 1994.
15. N. Paragios, P. Perez, G. Tziritas, C. Labit, and P. Bouthemy. Adaptive detection of moving objects using multiscale techniques. In *Proc. 3rd IEEE Int. Conf. Image Processing, ICIP'96*, Lausanne, Switzerland, September 1996.

16. P. Perez, A. Chardin, and J.M. Laferte. Noniterative manipulation of discrete energy-based models for image analysis. *PR*, 33(4):573–586, April 2000.
17. P.L. Rosin. Thresholding for change detection. *CVIU*, 86(2):79–95, May 2002.
18. E. Sifakis and G. Tziritas. Moving object localisation using a multi-label fast marching algorithm. *Signal Processing: Image Communication*, 16(10):963–976, 2001.
19. W.B. Thompson and T.C. Pong. Detecting moving objects. *IJCV*, 4(1):39–58, January 1990.

Appendix

Let us note V_{jk} the real velocity at the scale j at point $(2^{-j}k_1, 2^{-j}k_2)$.
$\exists(\lambda_1, \lambda_2)$ such as:

$$\frac{\lambda_1}{\lambda_1 + \lambda_2}||\vec{V}_{\epsilon^j} - \vec{V}|| \leq E(j,k,\Theta^j) \leq \sqrt{\frac{\lambda_2}{\lambda_1 + \lambda_2}}||\vec{V}_{\epsilon^j} - \vec{V}_{jk}|| \qquad (15)$$

with λ_1 and λ_2 respectively the smallest and the greatest eigenvalues

$$A = \begin{pmatrix} \sum\limits_{n=1}^{N} |\langle I, \frac{\partial \Psi_{jk}^n}{\partial x}\rangle|^2 & \sum\limits_{n=1}^{N} \langle I, \frac{\partial \Psi_{jk}^n}{\partial x}\rangle\langle I, \frac{\partial \Psi_{jk}^n}{\partial y}\rangle \\ \sum\limits_{n=1}^{N} \langle I, \frac{\partial \Psi_{jk}^n}{\partial x}\rangle\langle I, \frac{\partial \Psi_{jk}^n}{\partial y}\rangle & \sum\limits_{n=1}^{N} |\langle I, \frac{\partial \Psi_{jk}^n}{\partial y}\rangle|^2 \end{pmatrix}$$

Proof:

$$\sum_{n=1}^{N} ||\langle \vec{\nabla} I, \Psi_{jk}^n\rangle||^2 = \sum_{n=1}^{N} [|\langle I, \frac{\partial \Psi_{jk}^n}{\partial x}\rangle|^2 + |\langle I, \frac{\partial \Psi_{jk}^n}{\partial y}\rangle|^2]$$
$$= \text{trace}(A)$$
$$= \lambda_1 + \lambda_2$$

and as A is a symmetric positive definite matrix,

$$\lambda_1||X||^2 \leq X^T A X \leq \lambda_2||X||^2 \quad \forall X \qquad (16)$$

$\vec{V}_{jk}$ verifies:

$$\vec{\nabla}I.\vec{V}_{jk} = -\frac{\partial I}{\partial t}. \qquad (17)$$

Consequently,

$$E(j,k,\Theta^j) = \frac{\sum\limits_{n=1}^{N} ||\langle \vec{\nabla} I, \Psi_{jk}^n\rangle||.|\langle \vec{\nabla} I.(\vec{V}_{\epsilon^j} - \vec{V}_{jk}), \Psi_{jk}^n\rangle|}{\sum\limits_{n=1}^{N} ||\langle \vec{\nabla} I, \Psi_{jk}^n\rangle||^2}$$

And thanks to the Cauchy-Schwartz inequality,

$$E(j,k,\Theta^j) \leq \sqrt{\frac{\sum\limits_{n=1}^{N} |\langle \vec{\nabla} I.(\vec{V}_{\epsilon^j} - \vec{V}_{jk}), \Psi_{jk}^n\rangle|^2}{\sum\limits_{n=1}^{N} ||\langle \vec{\nabla} I, \Psi_{jk}^n\rangle||^2}}$$

Moreover,

$$
\begin{aligned}
\sum_{n=1}^{N} |\langle \overrightarrow{\nabla} I.(\overrightarrow{V}_{\epsilon^j} - \overrightarrow{V}_{jk}), \Psi_{jk}^n \rangle|^2 &= \sum_{n=1}^{N} |\langle I, \tfrac{\partial \Psi_{jk}^n}{\partial x} \rangle (V_{\epsilon^j} - V_{jk})_x + \langle I, \tfrac{\partial \Psi_{jk}^n}{\partial y} \rangle (V_{\epsilon^j} - V_{jk})_y|^2 \\
&= (\overrightarrow{V}_{\epsilon^j} - \overrightarrow{V}_{jk})^T A (\overrightarrow{V}_{\epsilon^j} - \overrightarrow{V}_{jk}) \\
&\le \lambda_2 \| \overrightarrow{V}_{\epsilon^j} - \overrightarrow{V}_{jk} \|^2
\end{aligned}
\tag{18}
$$

Thus:

$$
E(j, k, \Theta^j) \le \sqrt{\frac{\lambda_2}{\lambda_1 + \lambda_2}} \| \overrightarrow{V}_{\epsilon^j} - \overrightarrow{V}_{jk} \|
$$

And, according to the Minkowski inequality,

$$
\sum_{n=1}^{N} \| \langle \overrightarrow{\nabla} I, \Psi_{jk}^n \rangle \| . | \langle \overrightarrow{\nabla} I.(\overrightarrow{V}_{\epsilon^j} - \overrightarrow{V}_{jk}), \Psi_{jk}^n \rangle | \ge \| A.(\overrightarrow{V}_{\epsilon^j} - \overrightarrow{V}_{jk}) \| \ge \lambda_1 \| \overrightarrow{V}_{\epsilon^j} - \overrightarrow{V}_{jk} \|
$$

Consequently,

$$
E(j, k, \Theta^j) = \frac{\sum_{n=1}^{N} \| \langle \overrightarrow{\nabla} I, \Psi_{jk}^n \rangle \| . | \langle \overrightarrow{\nabla} I.(\overrightarrow{V}_{\epsilon^j} - \overrightarrow{V}_{jk}), \Psi_{jk}^n \rangle |}{\sum_{n=1}^{N} \| \langle \overrightarrow{\nabla} I, \Psi_{jk}^n \rangle \|^2} \ge \frac{\lambda_1}{\lambda_1 + \lambda_2} \| \overrightarrow{V}_{\epsilon^j} - \overrightarrow{V}_{jk} \|
$$

Segregation of Moving Objects
Using Elastic Matching

Vishal Jain, Benjamin B. Kimia, and Joseph L. Mundy

Division of Engineering,
Brown University, Providence, RI, USA
{vj, kimia, mundy}@lems.brown.edu

Abstract. We present a method for figure-ground segregation of moving objects from monocular video sequences. The approach is based on tracking extracted contour fragments, in contrast to traditional approaches which rely on feature points, regions, and unorganized edge elements. Specifically, a notion of similarity between pairs of curve fragments appearing in two adjacent frames is developed and used to find the curve correspondence. This similarity metric is elastic in nature and in addition takes into account both a novel notion of transitions in curve fragments across video frames and an epipolar constraint. This yields a performance rate of 85% correct correspondence on a manually labeled set of frame pairs. The retrieved curve correspondence is then used to group curves in each frame into clusters based on the pairwise similarity of how they transform from one frame to the next. Results on video sequences of moving vehicles show that using curve fragments for tracking produces a richer segregation of figure from ground than current region or feature-based methods.

1 Introduction

The key goal of this paper is to investigate tracking continuous edge curves in video sequences as a basis for figure-ground segmentation. The approach to be described here exploits the spatial continuity of contour fragments (connected edgel chains) in order to achieve more robust tracking and to obtain a more complete representation of the segmented moving object than produced by traditional optical-flow or point-based methods. The algorithm reported here is based on finding minimum energy curve deformation transformations from one frame to the next. Figure-ground classes are defined in terms of groups of curves transforming in a similar fashions as measured by curve matching distances.

The problem of object tracking in video has been extensively studied. The approaches can be loosely organized by the primary spatial dimension of the tracked feature, *i.e.* points [19, 11, 4, 24], curves [15, 13, 7, 14, 5, 8] or regions [16, 10, 20, 3, 6]. Point-based features are typically used in the context of 3D reconstruction, where points are matched across frames on the basis of Euclidean distance and image correlation in a local neighborhood around matching pairs. The epipolar constraint is used to eliminate erroneous matches using robust fitting algorithms such as RANSAC [12]. More recently, there has been considerable

W.J. MacLean (Ed.): SCVMA 2004, LNCS 3667, pp. 76–90, 2006.

interest in regions, where affine invariance derived from intensity operators [17] is used to define salient patches that can be recovered from multiple views of the same surface feature. These *affine patches* can be used for tracking as well as recognition.

Much of the prior literature on curve-based tracking exploits various types of deformable contours, such as polygons or cubic splines, which are tracked by optimizing image-based energy cost or likelihood functions. In most cases, these curves are initialized by hand in the first video frame. An early application of directly tracking edgels was demonstrated by Huttenlocker [13] who formed object templates from edge points and tracked them by minimizing the Hausdorff distance between point sets. However this work did not exploit the spatial continuity of the edge curves, which were treated as discrete point sets.

There seems to be little work on using connected edgel chains directly as the tracked representation. The closest work is that of Folta *et al.* [7], where they use edge curve matching to form the outlines of moving objects, the key objective of this paper. Our algorithmic approach is closest to that of Freedman [8] who considered curve tracking as a problem of optimum geometric alignment of detected intensity edges. A key difference from this paper is that Freedman assumes a *model* curve, which is supplied by hand initialization or by learning from a hand-picked set of example curves.

No such assumption is made in the current algorithm where curves, as segmented, are tracked across frames. In this regard, the tracking process is similar to that for points, *e.g.*, Harris corners, but in addition we exploit the order and continuity provided by segmented edgel chains. A key reason that edgel curves have not received much attention is that it difficult to define local correspondences between smooth curve segments. Here the correspondence problem is solved by exploiting both epipolar constraints from the object motion as well as optimizing global deformation energy. The epipolar constraint provides dense local matching constraints within global curve deformation energy that incorporates shape constraints of the entire curve.

The problem of tracking extracted edge contours in video appears straightforward but significant tracking complexity arises from the presence of smooth and discontinuous curve transformations and structural changes. An extracted curve can change smoothly over a number of frames but then undergo a singular visual event such as occlusion or a momentary specularity or fall below detection threshold. Under these discontinuous viewing conditions a curve can split, or merge with another curve, or simply disappear altogether. In practice, we expect 50-100 curve fragments from a typical frame and only about half depict smooth changes. The remaining set undergoes a *transition* as fully classified in Figure 1.

To understand the nature of deformations and topological evolution of image curves it is necessary to consider the underlying mechanisms that give rise to them. Image curves arise from discontinuities in the projection of 3D structure such as occluding contours (depth discontinuity), surface reflectance discontinuities, ridges on the object, illumination discontinuities (*e.g.*, highlights, shadows), and other effects. Movement of these curve fragments in a video sequence can

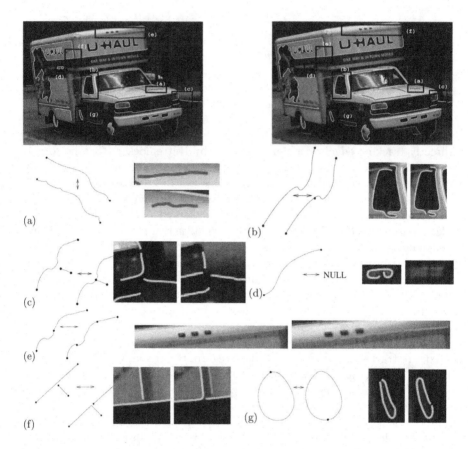

Fig. 1. Typical changes in curve fragments extracted from two frames of a video sequence using the topologically-driven edge operator [21] are illustrated for two frames of the UHAUL sequence. Typically, about half of curve fragments change smoothly as illustrated in (a). However, the remaining half can be expected to undergo abrupt changes as classified into six *transitions*: (b) a curve fragment can be split into two, or two can be joined into one. (c) The formation or disappearance of a T-junction. (d) The complete disappearance or appearance of a curve. (e) Compound fragmentation when two curve fragments join and split differently, a combination of two transitions of type "b". (f) Compound T-junction, a combination of transitions "c" and "b". (g) Compound fragmentation of closed curves, a combination of two transitions of type b.

in turn arise from changes in the viewpoint (*e.g.*, object or camera), illumination changes (*e.g.*, movement of light source) or inter-reflections on the moving object surface. Most of these effects lead to complex motions, which can only in the simplest cases be modeled. One tractable case is when the curves are due to fixed reflectance discontinuities on the moving object. In this case various approximations to perspective projection, *e.g.* planar affine motion, can provide a reasonable prediction of curve shape over time. However, for inter-reflections and occluding contours, there is no simple model to predict dynamic curve ge-

Fig. 2. The contour fragments of a moving vehicle are segregated from the background using only the two adjacent frames shown

ometry. As a final level of difficulty, outdoor scenes present a large intensity dynamic range which leads to fluctuating edge recovery from frame to frame. It is impossible to find edge detection parameters that will recover all the relevant edge segments as a moving object moves through shadows or is subject to specular refection.

Our approach relies on the following key observation: if each extracted curve fragment is sufficiently distinct from other extracted curves in the same frame, and if the inter-frame deformation for each curve fragment is small enough as compared to intra-frame curve differences, then the similarity between curve pairs in the two frames provides a basis for the recovery of curve correspondence by solving an assignment problem. However, the design of an effective similarity metric to capture both smooth and abrupt changes presents a challenge. We use an elastic matching metric based on the notion of an alignment curve that is symmetric in the order of the two curves matched [22] and modify it in three ways to address this issue. First, since only about half the curve fragments change smoothly, we modify the elastic metric to implicitly include a notion of curve transitions and use it to rank-order correspondence candidates. Second, transitions are explicitly handled so that broken curve fragments can be joined and the curve similarity matrix is suitably adjusted. Third, ambiguities arising from cases which violate our main assumption, *i.e.*, when the inter-frame curve distance is less than the intra-frame distance to their corresponding curves, are handled by bringing to bear a vanishing point constraint to spatially constrain the correspondence. The resulting similarity matrix is then converted into an assignment via a greedy best-first solution. We validated the resulting correspondence on a set of four labeled frame pair and noted improvements from an average correspondence rate of 48% for classical elastic matching to 56%, 68%, and 85%, respectively and cumulatively, for the three steps described above.

The recovered curve correspondence is the basis of figure-ground segregation. The main assumption is that curves belonging to the same object transform from one frame to another more similarity to each other than to curves from other objects or background. Specifically, from the inter-frame correspondence between each pair of curves a similarity transformation is recovered and a notion of transform similarity is defined between each pair of curves in a common frame.

This transform-induced similarity matrix is then converted into clusters which define objects and background in an image. The results on video frames of moving vehicles are very encouraging, as previewed in Figure 2, and are illustrated on a number of video sequence of moving vehicles later in this paper.

2   Curve Tracking Via Transition-Based Elastic Matching

In this section we describe a similarity-based method for finding the correspondence between contour fragments in two video frames. Specifically, we describe how contour fragments are extracted from each frame, how a correspondence is obtained from a pairwise elastic similarity of these curve fragments, and then describe three modifications to induce the notion of transitions and the vanishing point constraint.

Extracting Contours. The contour detector used in these experiments is based on a derivative of the Canny algorithm [2]. As is well known, the performance of the original Canny step edge detector is poor near corners and junctions. The algorithm developed in [21] focuses on extending the edgel chains at corners and junctions so that better topological connections are achieved by relaxing the constraints of the step edge model and searching for paths with the greatest intensity variation. The edges are located to sub-pixel accuracy using weighted parabolic interpolation with respect to the edge direction. Examples of these contour fragments are shown in Figure 1.

From a similarity metric to curve correspondence. The similarity metric S_{nm} is described below and is computed for curve fragments C_n and C_m, each from a different frame. The similarity matrix is converted into an *assignment* in a greedy best-first fashion. The highest similarity ranked pair in the matrix is made into a correspondence, and the remaining items in the corresponding row and column are removed to retain a one-to-one mapping. Furthermore, a second metric is used as an additional check on the similarity between this pair of curve fragments. Specifically, the optimal similarity transformation between the curves is obtained from the alignment, which is a key aspect of how the similarity between curves is computed, and the Hausdorff metric in the transform domain constitutes a second aspect of the similarity of the two curves. If this second metric does not indicate similarity beyond a threshold, this pair of highest ranked curve is disregarded. The process continues until either no rows or no columns remain. This greedy approach can be potentially further improved by achieving a globally optimal assignment, *e.g.*, by using graduated assignment [9, 23], but this is not the focus of this paper.

Transition-sensitive elastic Matching. We begin with an elastic curve-matching algorithm [22, 25] which minimizes an elastic energy functional over all possible alignments between two curves C and $\bar{C}$, by using an *alignment curve* α mediating between the two curves, Figure 3,

$$\alpha(\xi) = (h(\xi), \bar{h}(\xi)), \, \xi \in [0, \tilde{L}], \, \alpha(0) = (0,0), \, \alpha(\tilde{L}) = (L, \bar{L}), \qquad (1)$$

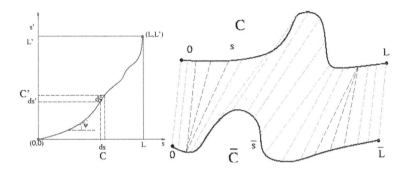

Fig. 3. From [22] The *alignment curve* (left) represents a correspondence between two curves (right). The notion of an alignment curve allows for predicting correspondences mapping an entire interval to a point; This aspect of the correspondence is crucial here as it does occur in the context of transitions. The optimal alignment curve α is efficiently found by dynamic programming [22].

where ξ is the arc-length along the alignment curve, h and $\bar{h}$ represent arc-lengths on C and $\bar{C}$, respectively, L and $\bar{L}$ represent lengths on C and $\bar{C}$, respectively, and $\tilde{L}$ is the length of the alignment curve α. The alignment curve can be specified by a single function, namely, $\psi(\xi)$, $\xi \in [0, \tilde{L}]$, where ψ denotes the angle between the tangent to the alignment curve and the x-axis. The arc-lengths of C and $\bar{C}$ can then be obtained by integration from ψ,

$$h(\xi) = \int_0^\xi \cos(\psi(\eta))d\eta, \ \bar{h}(\xi) = \int_0^\xi \sin(\psi(\eta))d\eta, \ \xi \in [0, \tilde{L}]. \qquad (2)$$

The optimal alignment α between the curves can be found by minimizing an energy functional μ,

$$\mu[\psi] = \int [|\cos(\psi) - \sin(\psi)| + R|\kappa(h)\cos(\psi) - \bar{\kappa}(\bar{h})\sin(\psi)|]d\xi \qquad (3)$$

where κ and $\bar{\kappa}$ are the curvatures of the curves. The first term describes differences in the arclength as defined in Eq 2 and thus penalizes "stretching". The second term is the difference in the angular extent associated with each infinitesimal pair of corresponding curve pieces and thus penalizes "bending" and R_1 relates the two terms. The "edit distance" between the curves C and $\bar{C}$ is defined as the cost of the optimal alignment given by $d(C, \bar{C}) = \min_\psi \mu(\psi)$ which is found by dynamic programming [22].

When this similarity metric is used to rank-order all curves in a frame with respect to a curve in another frame, the top ranking curve typically (72% for our database) yields the right correspondence when only gradual changes are involved. The overall curve correspondence performance is measured after the greedy assignment described earlier on a set of four manually labeled pairs of video frames. The overall curve-correspondence performance is 48% with errors arising mainly because transitions mislead the similarity metric, especially when

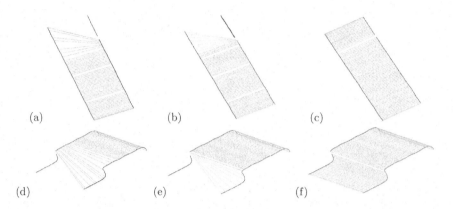

(a)   (b)   (c)

(d)   (e)   (f)

Fig. 4. (a,d) The elastic curve matching alignments are incorrect in the presence of a transition but modifying the energy function to allow for such cases corrects the alignment (b,e) and furthermore recovers the fragmented "tail". The alignment when excluding the tail is then used to define a geometric transform (similarity) between the two curves, which in turn is used to find and recover the broken curve fragment (c,f).

a portion of one curve is matched to an entire curve of which it is a fragment, Figure 4(a,d), *e.g.*, as occurs in the fragmentation transition, Figure 1(b).

Observe, however, that in such cases there often remains sufficient shape similarity information in the remaining portion to correctly identify it as a sub-curve of the other curve. This requires that the energy cost be appropriately modified to allow for the possibility of such transitions. The removal or addition of a contour segment during the match is represented as a vertical or horizontal segment in the beginning or in the end of the alignment curve, since either h is constant and $\bar{h}$ is varying, or vice-versa. To avoid discouraging such alignments, the elastic energy on these segments is diminished by a factor ν ($\nu = 0.3$ for all our experiments). Figure 4(b,e) illustrates that the alignment is correctly identified from a sub-curve to an entire curve, and this is typically the case when the fragment has sufficient structure on it. The significance of the above modification is twofold. First, the elastic energy arising from the new corrected alignment results in a corrected similarity measure which more often points to the correct corresponding curve. Second, it allows for a more precise similarity transformation since in the corrected alignment the "tails" mapping an entire segment to a point are discarded from the Hausdorff distance computation, which is more sensitive to the presence of "tails". This modification of the energy functional aimed at handling sub-curve matching increases the performance from 48% to 56%.

Explicit handling of transitions. The above modification works well for sub-curves which have sufficient shape content but not so well for smaller sub-curves. Thus, in stage two we explicitly use the structure of the transition in the form of joint matching. Specifically, assuming that the first stage has been successful in identifying the right correspondence for one of the sub-curves involved in the transition, the existence of a "tail" in the alignment (as shown in Figures 4(b,e)) indicates that a transition has likely occurred. Recall that the similarity transformation between the two curve fragments is obtained in the verification step without involving the initial "tail". We now transform the "tail" accordingly in search of a mate in the other frame. If a third curve exists that is sufficiently similar, the two sub-curves are merged and identified as a single curve, Figure 1(c-f). While this can be done iteratively for multiply fragmented curves, our current implementation only joins two curve fragments. With this improvement correspondence performance increases from 56% to about 68%.

Use of Epipolar constraint to reduce ambiguity. The above transition-sensitive shape-based similarity fails in two cases. First, when numerous similar structures are present, as in the seven rectangles in the front grill of the vehicle in Figure 5(a), the alignment between any pair of curve fragments is excellent and of low energy, so that the intrinsic nature of this shape metric does not significantly differentiate them to rank-order matches according to extrinsic placement. The second case involves contours which do not have significant "shape content", as in the straight lines on the pavement in Figure 5(b), so that there are numerous curve fragments with nearly equivalent alignments and energies. In such cases it is useful to introduce an extrinsic measure, namely, the *epipolar constraint*. We assume that within a limited neighborhood of frames, the motion of the object giving rise to the curve can be approximated as a translation, requiring the alignments between projected curves to pass through an epipole **e**, Figure 6. This epipole is either available as a vanishing point of the scene or it can be estimated together with the alignment between a pair of curves. In our experiments the camera was fixed, so the edges on the road are used to find the vanishing point manually.

The epipolar constraint is incorporated in the curve energy using an epipolar term. Consider a point of the alignment curve relating point P_1 on the first curve to the point P_2 on the second curve, Figure 6. Then distance of the point P_2 from the epipolar line passing through P_1 is computed along the tangent direction of P_2. The tangential distance d_e is estimated from the perpendicular

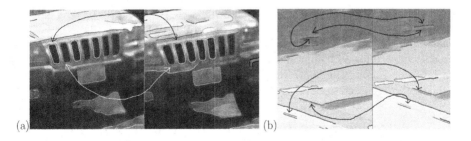

(a)   (b)

Fig. 5. The stage two similarity metric fails to identify the corresponding pair when multiple similar structures exist (a) or when curves do not depict significant structure (b)

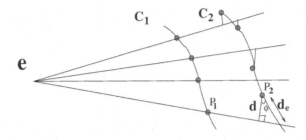

Image-pair	% correct
SUV67-68	80
PoliceCar16-17	86
PoliceCar21-22	86
Minivan65-66	90

Fig. 6. Epipolar lines through the sample points of the first curve should pass closely to the corresponding sample points on the second point, and vice versa. The distances between these corresponding points and the lines through he original sample points indicate deviation from the epipolar constraint and is used as an addition clue towards finding the correct curve correspondence.

Fig. 7. Curve correspondence results for four manually labeled image-pairs

distance d using $d_e = \frac{d}{cos\phi}$, where ϕ is angle between the tangent at point P_2 and the perpendicular line to the epipolar line as shown in Figure 6. Similarily a second estimate of d_e is computed with the role of the points based P_1 and P_2 reversed and the maximum is used as the values of d_e. The modified energy then takes the form

$$\mu[\psi] = \int [|\cos(\psi) - \sin(\psi)| + R_1 |\kappa(h)\cos(\psi) - \bar{\kappa}(\bar{h})\sin(\psi)| + R_2 |(d_e)^p/(1+(d_e)^p)|]d\xi,$$

where $p = 10$. The performance after this stage increases from 68% to 85%.

Results. Figures 8 shows several examples of the final curve correspondence for adjacent frames taken from several video sequences. In order to formally evaluate the curve correspondence algorithm, a database of ground truth consisting of four image pairs was manually created. Along with this, a curve is also labelled as foreground or background for verification of results in Section 3. As tabulated in Figure 7, 80%-90% of correspondences are correct in these four frames which, as we shall see in the next section, is sufficiently high to enable reliable figure-ground segregation. We also expect significant improvements when several other constraints are utilized in the similarity measure, including a measure of intensity and color match for each alignment, use of 3D geometric reconstruction, imposing spatial order among the curve fragments to disambiguate correspondences, and in particular when compound transitions are also explicitly handled.

3   Transformation-Induced Figure-Ground Segregation

In this section we describe a figure-ground segregation method based on the Gestalt cue of *common fate*. Specifically, since the curve correspondence has established how each curve transforms form one frame to another, curves with distinctly sim-

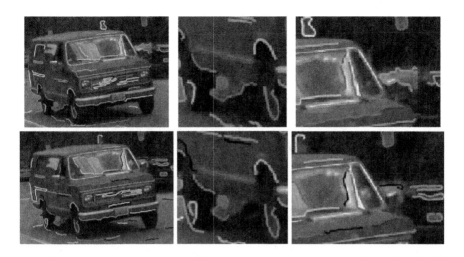

Fig. 8. Matched curves in a pair of video frames (top and bottom, on the left) and corresponding zoomed areas on the right. Corresponding curve fragments are shown in the same color.

ilar transforms should be grouped. These transforms are characterized in the domain of an expected geometric transform, in our case the similarity transform, although affine or projective transformations can also be used. While it is tempting to measure the similarity between two transforms by measuring the distance between the parameter vectors describing each transform, it is much more meaningful to measure similarity not in the parameter space, but in the observation space. Specifically, a transform $T_1(T_{1x}, T_{1y}, \theta_1, \lambda_1)$ where (T_{1x}, T_{1y}) are translation coordinates and θ_1 is the angle of rotation, and λ_1 is scaling is defined by an inter-frame curve pair $(C_1, \bar{C}_1)$ and similarly $T_2(T_{2x}, T_{2y}, \theta_2, \lambda_2)$ is defined for the $(C_2, \bar{C}_2)$ pair. Rather than rely on differences between the parameter describing T_1 and T_2, we defined the similarity of T_1 and T_2 by the extent T_1C_2 is similar as a curve to $\bar{C}_2$, and analogously, T_2C_1 is similar to $\bar{C}_1$, Figure 9,

$$d_T(C_1, C_2) = max\{d_H(T_1C_2, \bar{C}_2), d_H(T_2C_1, \bar{C}_1)\}. \qquad (4)$$

where d_H is the Hausdorff metric between two curves.

Image-pair	object curves	false segre-gation	recovered curves
SUV67-68	84	4	53
PoliceCar16-17	38	3	19
PoliceCar21-22	31	5	16
Minivan65-66	65	4	31

Fig. 9. Green curves in frame 2 are modeled similarity transformations of the red curves in frame 1 while blue curves are the actual curves in frame 2

Fig. 10. Segregation results for four manually labeled image pairs

This pairwise measure defines the degree by which two curves in one frame have common fate with respect to the second frame and is represented by an $m \times m$ matrix where m is the number of curves in the first frame. Ideally, a moving object on a stationary background would lead to two distinct clusters in this matrix. However, since background curves can also shift in a wide range of movements resembling some of those on the object, *e.g.*, tree branches moving in the wind, this distinction is smeared.

We adopt a simple clustering technique to determine cluster boundaries, namely, the seeded region growing method used for segmentation of intensity images [1]. Each curve is initialized as a cluster. The distance between two

Fig. 11. Results of Figure-ground segregation based on two adjacent frames for a Van (first frame shown on the left) and an SUV(first frame shown on the right). The top row shows the original image, the second row shows the contours extracted and last row shows the segmented object.

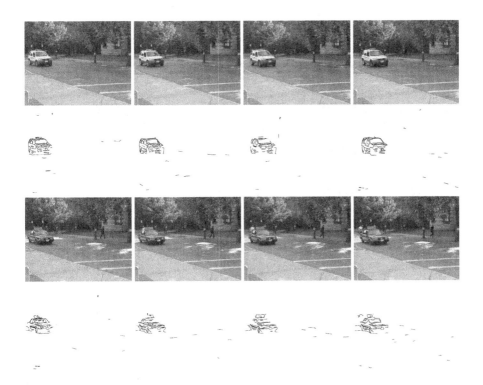

Fig. 12. Two-frame segregation of moving vehicles in two subsequent video sequences

clusters is defined as the median of pairwise distances between their members. An iterative procedure then merges the two closest clusters into one until either the closest distance between clusters exceeds some threshold or the number of clusters falls below a minimum number of expected clusters. Figure 11 depicts the clusters associated with the foreground for two distinct frame pairs. Figures 12 show examples for four subsequent frames, but each using the method on an adjacent pair of frames only. As tabulated in Figure 10 the segregation includes few non-object contours (5%-10%) for our four ground-truth frame pairs, while capturing a significant collection of the curves on the object.

The computational complexity of the approach depends on a number of factors including the number of curves and the number of sample points on each curve. There are generally 200-300 curve fragments per frame. The number of sample points on each curve varies from 40 to 200. The complexity of matching a pair of curve segments is $O(n^2)$ where n is the number of sample points on curve segments but multiscale approaches can be used to speed this up. The complexity for matching curves in two frame is $O(M^2n^2)$ where M is the number of curves in a frame. The overall analysis takes approximately 2 to 2.5 minutes to process a frame on Pentium 4, 2 GHz machine.

88   V. Jain, B.B. Kimia, and J.L. Mundy

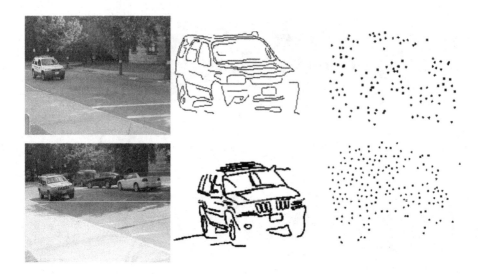

Fig. 13. Comparison of our results with the KLT tracker [24]. Observe how our segregation produces a richer description of the figure which can than be used for recognition.

There are several system parameters: τ is the threshold for the edge-detector (default value is 1.5); e is the initial estimate of the epipole which is currently estimated manually but which will be automatically estimated in the matching process in the future; N is the initial number of clusters and d_{min} is the minimum inter-distance cluster for the clustering algorithm; ν is the energy factor reduction for end-points of the curve (default value is 0.3); and, R_1 and R_2 are the constants used in the cost function (default values are 10 and 3 respectively).

We emphasize that these results while already very encouraging are only using pairwise comparison of frames and can be potentially significantly improved further. Observe in Figure 12 how each frame pair gives a segmentation that has many common curve fragments with its nearby frame pairs, but also feature novel curves not seen before. We have not yet utilized this *multi-frame regularity* which should lead to a dense and complete segmentation after a few frames. Also, the emphasis has not been on using a sophisticated clustering method, although the use of one would certainly improve the results. The use of color and contrast as an attribute of each curve as was done for puzzle matching [18] will likely improve the selectivity if the curve matching processing the future. We expect that the addition of regional motion information will also significantly improve the results. As the comparison in Figure 13 shows our curve-based approach is a promising direction for figure-ground segregation and tracking in a wide range of applications.

Acknowledgements. This research was funded in part by DARPA contract #NBCH-1-03-0006.

References

1. R. Adams and L. Bischof. Seeded region growing. *PAMI*, 16(6):641–647, 1994.
2. J. Canny. A computational approach to edge detection. *PAMI*, 8:679–698, 1986.
3. D. Comaniciu, V. Ramesh, and P. Meer. Real-time tracking of nonrigid objects using mean shift. In *Proc. IEEE Conf. on CVPR*, pages 2:142–149, Hilton Head Island, South Carolina, 2000.
4. R. Deriche and G. Giraudon. A computational approach for corner and vertex detection. *IJCV*, pages 167–187, 1993.
5. C. E. Erdem, A. Tekalp, and B. Sankur. Video object tracking with feedback of performance measures. In *Proc. IEEE conference on CVPR*, pages 593–600, Dec 2001.
6. V. Ferrari, T. Tuytelaars, and L. van Gool. Real-time affine region tracking and coplanar grouping. In *Proc. IEEE Conf. on CVPR*, pages 226–233, Kauai, Hawaii, 2001.
7. F. Folta, L. V. Eycken, and L. van Gool. Shape extraction using temporal continuity. In *Proc. European Workshop on Image Analysis for Multimedia Interactive Services of the IEEE conference on CVPR*, pages 69–74, 1997.
8. D. Freedman. Effective tracking through tree search. In *IEEE Trans. on PAMI*, volume 25, pages 604–615, May 2003.
9. S. Gold, A. Rangarajan, and E. Mjolsness. Learning with preknowledge:clustering with point and graph matching distance measures. *Neural Computation*, 8(4):787–804, 1996.
10. G. Hager and P. Belhumeur. Efficient region tracking with parametric models of geometry and illumination. *PAMI*, 20(10):1025–1039, 1998.
11. C. Harris. Determination of ego-motion from matched points. *IJCV*, pages 189–192, 1993.
12. R. Hartley and A. Zisserman. *Multiple View Geometry in Computer Vision*. Cambridge University Press, 2000.
13. D. P. Huttenlocher, G. A. Klanderman, and W. J. Rucklidge. Comparing images using the Hausdorff distance. *PAMI*, 15:850–863, 1993.
14. M. Isard and A. Blake. Condensation - conditional density propagation for visual tracking. *IJCV*, pages 29:2–28, 1998.
15. M. Kass, A. Witkin, and D. Terzopoulos. Snakes: Active contour models. *International Journal of Computer Vision*, 1(4):321–331, 1987.
16. D. Koller, J. Weber, and J. Malik. Robust multiple car tracking with occlusion reasoning. In *Proceedings of the Third European Conference on Computer Vision*, volume I. Springer Verlag, 1994.
17. T. Lindenberg. Feature detection with automatic scale detection. *IJCV*, 30(2):77–116, 1998.
18. J. McBride. Archaeological fragment reassembly using curve matching. Master's dissertation, Brown University, Providence,USA, 2003.
19. H. P. Moravec. Visual mapping by a robot rover. In *Proc. of the 6th International Joint Conference on Artificial Intelligence*, pages 598–600, 1979.
20. N. Paragios and R. Deriche. A pde-based level set approach for detection and tracking of moving objects. In *Proc. IJCV*, Bombay,India, Jan 1998.
21. C. Rothwell, J. Mundy, W. Hoffman, and V.-D. Nguyen. Driving vision by topology. In *IEEE Intl. Symosium on Computer Vision*, pages 395–400, 1995.

22. T. Sebastian, P. Klein, and B. Kimia. On aligning curves. *IEEE Trans. PAMI*, 25(1):116–125, January 2003.
23. D. Sharvit, J. Chan, H. Tek, and B. B. Kimia. Symmetry-based indexing of image databases. *JVCIR*, 9(4):366–380, December 1998.
24. J. Shi and C. Tomasi. Good features to track. In *Proc. of the IEEE conference on CVPR*, pages 593–600, 1994.
25. L. Younes. Computable elastic distance between shapes. *SIAM Journal of Applied Mathematics*, 58:565–586, 1998.

Local Descriptors for Spatio-temporal Recognition*

Ivan Laptev and Tony Lindeberg

Computational Vision and Active Perception Laboratory (CVAP),
Dept. of Numerical Analysis and Computing Science,
KTH, S-100 44 Stockholm, Sweden

Abstract. This paper presents and investigates a set of local space-time descriptors for representing and recognizing motion patterns in video. Following the idea of local features in the spatial domain, we use the notion of space-time interest points and represent video data in terms of local space-time events. To describe such events, we define several types of image descriptors over local spatio-temporal neighborhoods and evaluate these descriptors in the context of recognizing human activities. In particular, we compare motion representations in terms of spatio-temporal jets, position dependent histograms, position independent histograms, and principal component analysis computed for either spatio-temporal gradients or optic flow. An experimental evaluation on a video database with human actions shows that high classification performance can be achieved, and that there is a clear advantage of using local position dependent histograms, consistent with previously reported findings regarding spatial recognition.

1 Introduction

When performing recognition from spatial or spatio-temporal images, the definition of the underlying image representation is of crucial importance for subsequent recognition. During recent years there has been a substantial progress on recognition schemes that are based on either local or global image features. In particular, the use of view-based approaches in terms of receptive field responses [10] has emerged as a highly promising approach for visual recognition.

When performing recognition, global methods are conceptually simple to implement. For complex scenes with occlusions and multiple moving objects, however, such methods require a complementary segmentation step, which may be non-trivial to achieve in practice. In this respect, local approaches have an interesting potential, while requiring a complementary matching step between the local features in the model and the data. For a recognition scheme to be invariant to size changes in the image domain as well as temporal phenomena

---

* The support from the Swedish Research Council and from the Royal Swedish Academy of Sciences as well as the Knut and Alice Wallenberg Foundation is gratefully acknowledged. We also thank Christian Schüldt and Barbara Caputo for their help in obtaining the experimental video data.

W.J. MacLean (Ed.): SCVMA 2004, LNCS 3667, pp. 91–103, 2006.

that occur with different speed, it is natural to require the image descriptors to be invariant to spatial and temporal scale changes. Similarly, in order to handle unknown relative motions between the objects and the camera, invariance to local Galilean transformations can be expected to be a highly useful property.

In the area of motion-based recognition, a large number of different schemes have been developed based on various combinations of visual tasks and image descriptors; see e.g. the monograph by [24] and the survey paper by [7] for overviews of early works. Concerning more recent approaches, [1, 25] performed tracking and recognition using principal component analysis and parameterized models of optic flow. [8] presented a related approach using Zernike polynomial expansions of optic flow. [2] recognized human actions against a static background by computing templates of temporal differences and characterizing the resulting motion masks in terms of moments. [3, 26] recognized activities using probabilistic models of spatio-temporal receptive fields while [13] extended this approach to histograms of locally velocity-adapted receptive fields. Another statistical, non-parametric approach for motion recognition in terms of temporal multiscale Gibbs models was proposed by [5]. [4] presented a recognition scheme in terms of positive and negative components of stabilized optic flow in spatio-temporal volumes.

Space-time interest points [11] have recently been proposed to capture local events in video. Such points have stable locations in space-time and provide a potential basis for part-based representations of complex motions in video. The subject of this paper, is to study different ways of defining local space-time descriptors associated with such interest points and to use these descriptors for subsequent recognition of spatio-temporal events and activities. The approach can hence be seen as an extension of previous interest point based spatial recognition approaches [17, 19] into space-time.

In previous works in the spatial domain, it has been shown that the use of automatic scale selection allows for the computation of scale invariant image descriptors [14, 17, 19, 6], and that the SIFT descriptor [17], which can be seen as a scale-adapted position dependent histogram of spatial gradient vectors, is very powerful for spatial recognition [20]. Moreover, histograms of spatial or spatio-temporal derivatives have been shown to allow for spatial and spatio-temporal recognition [22, 26]. For handling perspective as well as Galilean image deformations, affine shape adaptation [16, 19] and velocity adaptation [21, 15, 13] have been demonstrated to be useful mechanisms.

In this paper, we shall combine and connect these types of mechanisms into new types of powerful spatio-temporal image descriptors. Specifically, we shall compare local space-time descriptors at interest points in terms of various combinations of N-jets, optic flow, principal component analysis as well as local histograms with or without spatial dependency. We will show that such local descriptors allow for matching of spatio-temporal events and activities between image sequences. The performance will be measured by evaluating classification rates on a video database with different types of human activities.

2   Spatio-temporal Interest Points

Following [11], let us adopt a local interest point approach for capturing spatio-temporal events in video data. Consider an image sequence f and construct a spatio-temporal scale-space representation L by convolution with a spatio-temporal Gaussian kernel $g(x, y, t; \sigma, \tau) = 1/(2\pi\sigma^2\sqrt{2\pi}\tau)\exp(-(x^2+y^2)/2\sigma^2 - t^2/2\tau^2)$ with spatial and temporal scale parameters σ and τ. Then, at any point $p = (x, y, t)$ in space-time define a spatio-temporal second-moment matrix μ as

$$\mu(p) = \int_{q \in \mathbb{R}^3} (\nabla L(q))(\nabla L(q))^T g(p - q; \sigma_i, \tau_i)\, dq, \tag{1}$$

where $\nabla L = (L_x, L_y, L_t)^T$ denotes the spatio-temporal gradient vector and $(\sigma_i = \gamma\sigma, \tau_i = \gamma\tau)$ are spatial and temporal integration scales with $\gamma = \sqrt{2}$. Neighborhoods with μ of rank 3 correspond to points with significant variations of image values over both space and time. Points that maximize these variations can be detected by maximizing all eigenvalues $\lambda_1, .., \lambda_3$ of μ or, similarly, by searching the maxima of the interest point operator $H = \det\mu - k(\text{trace}\,\mu)^2 = \lambda_1\lambda_2\lambda_3 - k(\lambda_1 + \lambda_2 + \lambda_3)^3$ over (x, y, t) subject to $H \geq 0$ with $k \approx 0.005$.

Scale selection. To estimate the spatial and the temporal extents (σ_0, τ_0) of events, we maximize the following normalized feature strength measure over spatial and temporal scales [14, 11] at each detected interest point $p_0 = (x_0, y_0, t_0)$

$$(\sigma_0, \tau_0) = \operatorname*{argmax}_{\sigma, \tau}(\sigma^2\tau^{1/2}(L_{xx} + L_{yy}) + \sigma\tau^{3/2}L_{tt})^2. \tag{2}$$

Velocity adaptation. Moreover, to compensate for (generally unknown) relative motion between the camera and the moving pattern, we perform velocity adaptation [21, 15, 13, 12] by locally warping the neighborhoods of each interest point with a Galilean transformation using image velocity u estimated by computing optic flow [18] at the interest point.

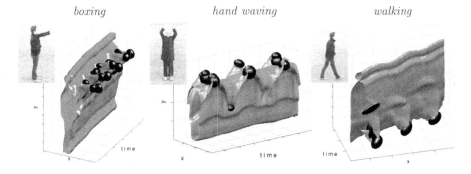

boxing   *hand waving*   *walking*

Fig. 1. Examples of scale and Galilean adapted spatio-temporal interest points. The illustrations show one image from the image sequence and a level surface of image brightness over space-time with the space-time interest points illustrated as dark ellipsoids.

Figure 1 shows a few examples of spatio-temporal interest points computed in this way from image sequences with human activities. As can be seen, the method allows us to extract scale-adaptive regions of interest around spatio-temporal events in a manner that is invariant to spatial and temporal scale changes as well as to local Galilean transformations.

3   Space-Time Image Descriptors at Interest Points

The subject of this section is to present a set of image descriptors to characterize the local space-time structure around interest points for subsequent recognition.

3.1   Image Measurements

As basis for defining spatio-temporal image descriptors, we shall make use of image measurements in terms of either:

- *Gaussian derivatives* up order four computed by applying scale normalized spatial and temporal derivatives [14] to the scale-space representation L

$$\mathcal{J}_{norm}\left(g(\cdot;\ \sigma_0, \tau_0) * f\right) = \{\sigma L_x, \sigma L_y, \tau L_t, \sigma^2 L_{xx}, \ldots, \sigma \tau^3 L_{yttt}, \tau^4 L_{tttt}\} \quad (3)$$

  at locally adapted scale levels (σ_0, τ_0) as obtained from the scale selection step when detecting spatio-temporal interest points (see Fig. 2(left)). Specifically, we shall consider two types of Gaussian derivative descriptors; (i) the local (pointwise) N-jets [10] of order $N = 4$ evaluated at an interest point, and (ii) a multi-local gradient vector field obtained by evaluating the jet of order one at every point in a local neighborhood of an interest point.
- *Optic flow* computed from second-moment matrices around the space-time interest points, according to the method by Lukas and Kanade [18], and at locally adapted scale levels determined from the space-time interest points.

Due to the scale normalization in combination with the scale selection procedure, the N-jets will be scale invariant over both space and time [14, 11]. Scale invariance of the optic flow is achieved by computing the optic flow using scale-normalized Gaussian derivatives at locally adapted scale levels. For the purpose of Galilean invariance, both the N-jet and the optic flow are computed from locally warped space-time volumes as obtained from the velocity adaptation procedure.

There are a number of qualitative similarities as well as differences between these two types of image measurements: The N-jet contains a truncated encoding of the complete space-time image structure around the interest point, with an implicit encoding of the optic flow. By explicitly computing the optic flow, we obtain a representation that is invariant to local contrast in the image domain, at the cost of possible errors in the flow estimation step. In addition to the optic flow, the N-jet also encodes the local spatial structure, which may either help or distract the recognition scheme depending on the relation between the contents in the training and the testing data. Hence, it is of interest to investigate both types of image measurements.

3.2   Types of Image Descriptors

Then, we combine these measurements into image descriptors by considering:

– *Histograms* of either spatio-temporal gradients or optic flow computed at several scales. The histograms will be computed either for the entire neighborhood of an interest point, or over several ($M \times M \times M$) smaller neighborhoods around the interest point. For the latter case, here referred to as position dependent histograms, local coordinates are measured relative to the detected interest points and are used in the descriptors together with local image measurements (see Fig. 2(right)). Local measurements are weighted using Gaussian window function where we for simplicity marginalize the histograms and compute separable histograms over either the components of spatio-temporal gradients or the components of optic flow.
– *Principal component analysis* (PCA) of either optic flow or spatio-temporal gradient vectors (L_x, L_y, L_t) computed over local scale and velocity normalized spatio-temporal neighborhoods around the interest points. The principal components are computed from space-time interest points extracted from training data, and the data is then projected to a lower-dimensional space with D dimensions defined by the most significant eigenvectors (see Fig. 2(middle)).

Space-time derivative filters   PCA basis gradient fields   Position-dependent histograms

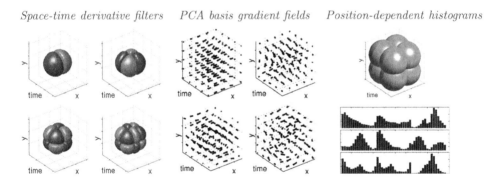

Fig. 2. (left) Examples N-jet components in terms of partial spatio-temporal derivative operators, here: $\partial_x, \partial_{xt}, \partial_{xyt}, \partial_{xxyt}$. (middle) Examples of basis vectors obtained by performing PCA on spatio-temporal gradients around space-time interest points. (right) Examples of position dependent histograms (bottom) computed using overlapping window functions (top).

3.3   Spatio-temporal Image Descriptors

By combining the abovementioned notions in different ways, we will consider the following types of space-time image descriptors:

1. N-jet of order 4 at a single scale, computed at (x_0, y_0, t_0) at scale (σ_0, τ_0).
2. Multi-scale N-jet of order 4, computed at all 9 combinations of 3 spatial scales $(\sigma_0/2, \sigma_0, 2\sigma_0)$ and 3 temporal scales $(\tau_0/2, \tau_0, 2\tau_0)$ at (x_0, y_0, t_0).

3. Local position dependent histograms of first-order partial derivatives.
4. Local position independent histograms of first-order partial derivatives.
5. Local position dependent histograms of optic flow.
6. Local position independent histograms of optic flow.
7. Local principal component analysis of optic flow.
8. Local principal component analysis of spatio-temporal gradients vectors.
9. Global histograms of first-order partial spatio-temporal derivatives computed over the entire image sequence using 9 combinations of 3 spatial scales and 3 temporal scales. This descriptor is closely related to [26] and is mainly considered here as a reference with respect to the previous global schemes for spatio-temporal recognition.

To obtain affine contrast invariance, the N-jets as well as the spatio-temporal gradient vectors are normalized to unit l_2-norm. For the principal component analysis of spatio-temporal gradient fields, the affine contrast normalization is performed at the level of scale normalized image volumes.

For an interest point detected at position (x_0, y_0, t_0) and scale (σ_0, τ_0), all histograms were computed at all 9 combinations of 3 spatial scales $(\sigma_0/2, \sigma_0, 2\sigma_0)$ and 3 temporal scales $(\tau_0/2, \tau_0, 2\tau_0)$. The global histograms were computed at combinations of spatial scales $\sigma \in \{1, 2, 4\}$ and temporal scales $\tau \in \{1, 2, 4\}$. When accumulating histograms of spatio-temporal gradients, only image points with L_t above a threshold were allowed to contribute. Moreover, all histograms were smoothed with a binomial filter and were normalized to unit l_1-norm. For the position dependent histograms (Descriptors 3 and 5), we initially consider $M = 2$ and evaluate the position dependent entities using Gaussian weighted window functions centered at $(x_0 \pm \alpha\sigma_0, y_0 \pm \alpha\sigma_0, t_0 \pm \beta\tau_0)$ with $\alpha = 1.5$ and $\beta = 1.5$. The spatial standard deviation of the Gaussian weighting function was 3σ and the temporal standard deviation 3τ. For the position dependent histograms, 16 bins were used for the components of the spatio-temporal gradients or the optic flow, while 32 bins were used for the position independent histograms. Thus, with $M = 2$ the position dependent histograms contain 9 scales × 8 positions × 3 derivatives × 16 bins = 3456 accumulator cells, and position independent histograms contain 9 scales × 3 derivatives × 32 bins = 864 cells. For the local principal component analysis, the gradient vectors and the optic flow were computed in windows of spatial extent $\pm 3\sigma$ and temporal extent $\pm 3\tau$ around the interest points. Prior to the computation of principal components using $D = 100$ dimensions, the gradient vectors and the optic flow were resampled to a 9 × 9 × 9 grid using trilinear interpolation.

These descriptors build upon several previous works. The use of the N-jet for expressing visual operations was proposed by [10] and the first application to spatio-temporal recognition was presented in [3]. The use of histograms of receptive field responses goes back to [22, 26], and the use of PCA for optic flow was proposed by [1]. The use of complementary position information in histograms is closely related to the position dependency in the SIFT descriptor [17]. Recently, [9] added a local principal component analysis to the SIFT descriptor.

Hence, Descriptors 1, 2, 4, 6 and 7 can be seen as adaptations (and combinations) of previous approaches to space-time interest points, Descriptor 9 can be seen as a variation of [26], while Descriptors 3, 5 and 8 are basically new, although with qualitative relations to some of the abovementioned works.

4   Matching

For recognizing spatio-temporal events and activities, we shall in this section explore the idea of matching space-time interest points attributed with image descriptors according to section 3.

Video database with human activities. For testing and evaluating our methods, we shall use a video database with 192 image sequences, with 8 people performing 6 types of actions ("walking", "jogging", "running", "boxing", "handclapping", "handwaving"). Each action is repeated four times by each subject, and for the cases of "walking", "jogging" and "running", there are two sequences where the subject is moving leftwards and two sequences with the subject moving rightwards (see figure 4 for a few sample image sequences for each type of activity).

Similarity/dissimilarity measures. For comparing descriptors h_1 and h_2 at different interest points, we consider the following similarity/dissimilarity measures:

- Normalized scalar product: $S(h_1, h_2) = \frac{\sum_i h_1(i) h_2(i)}{\sqrt{\sum_i h_1^2(i)} \sqrt{\sum_i h_2^2(i)}}$

- Euclidean distance: $E(h_1, h_2) = \sum_i (h_1(i) - h_2(i))^2$

- The χ^2-measure: $\chi^2(h_1, h_2) = \sum_i \frac{(h_1(i) - h_2(i))^2}{h_1(i) + h_2(i)}$

For descriptors in terms of N-jets, the feature vector h consists of Gaussian derivatives at an adaptively determined set of spatio-temporal scales. For the histogram descriptors, the feature vector is defined from the contents of all the accumulator cells. For PCA descriptors, the feature vector consists of projections of local image measurements onto D principal components.

Matching space-time interest points and image sequences. For matching local space-time features between image sequences, we will use a local greedy method. Given that the K strongest interest points have been computed in a training and a testing image, the similarity (dissimilarity) measure is evaluated for each pair of features. The pair with maximum similarity (or minimum dissimilarity) is matched and the corresponding features are removed from the training and testing sets. The procedure is repeated until no more feature pairs can be matched, either due to a threshold on similarity (dissimilarity) or lack of data.

Figure 3 shows a few examples of space-time interest points matched in this way for pairs of image sequences. As can be seen, many interest points identify the same type of events in different sequences disregarding variations in scale, cloth, lightning and complex backgrounds. To define similarity (dissimilarity) measures for pairs of sequences, we sum the individual similarities (dissimilarities) obtained from m best point matches. Of course, one could also consider

Correct matches: changes in scale, cloth, light, background   *False matches*

Fig. 3. Examples of point matches of space-time interest points using local image descriptors in terms of position dependent histograms of spatio-temporal gradient vectors

adding these measures transformed by a monotonically increasing function. Figure 4 shows a few examples of performing matching between image sequences in the database. As can be seen, the types of actions in the matched sequences (on the right) correspond to the actions in the test sequences (in the left column).

5   Experiments

To evaluate the performance of the different types of image descriptors, we will perform leave-X-out experiments for random perturbations of the database. In other words, the image sequences for X of the subjects will be removed from the database to be used as testing data, while the remaining image sequences will be used as training data. Then, for each image sequence in the test set, a best match is determined among all the image sequences in the training set. A match

Fig. 4. One sequence for each type of action in the database [23] with its best sorted matches (ordered from left to right). Here, all matches are correct except for the sequence with "running" for which the fourth best match is "jogging".

is regarded as correct if the activity of the best match in the training set agrees with the activity of the image sequence in the test set.

Figure 5 shows the result of computing classification rates in this way for the different types of image descriptors defined in section 3.3 using different types of similarity (dissimilarity) measures presented in section 4. For those descriptors that involve free parameters to be determined, we only show the results for the best parameters that were tested. The χ^2-measure is evaluated only for histogram-based descriptors.

As can be seen, for all three types of error metrics the position dependent histograms give the best results. Specifically, the position dependent histograms give better results than corresponding position independent histograms, both for spatio-temporal gradients and optic flow. Moreover, the position dependent histograms give better results than a principal component analysis of corresponding descriptors. In addition, most of our local methods give better re-

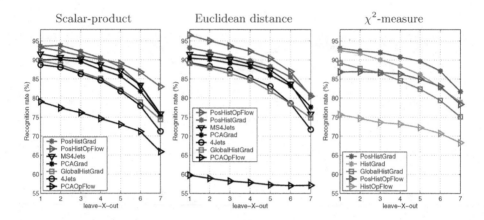

Fig. 5. Classification rates for different types of space-time image descriptors in leave-X-out experiments using either (a) normalized scalar product as similarity measure, (b) Euclidean distance as dissimilarity measure or (c) χ^2 dissimilarity measure. The results are averages over random permutations of the database. Specific comparison between position dependent histograms and position independent histograms for the χ^2 measure in (c) demonstrates the advantage of using position dependent histograms. Qualitatively similar results were obtained for the two other measures (left out here).

sults than the global histogram method. The multi-scale N-jet performs better than a principal component analysis of spatio-temporal gradient vectors or optic flow, and a multi-scale N-jet gives better results than a corresponding single-scale jet. We also evaluated recognition using N-jets of order two, but the performance of the forth order N-jets was slightly better. Position-dependent histograms with $M = 3$ were tested as well but did not give significant improvement.

Currently, the best results are obtained using position dependent histograms of optic flow in combination with a Euclidean distance measure. The second best method is a position dependent histogram of spatio-temporal gradients in combination with the normalized scalar product. The third best image descriptor out of these is the multi-scale N-jet, both for the case of using a normalized scalar

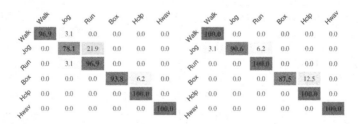

Fig. 6. Confusion matrices when classifying human activities with local descriptors in terms of position dependent histograms of spatio-temporal gradients (left) and optic flow (right)

product or the Euclidean distance as error metric. A conceptual advantage of the multi-scale N-jet is that it is essentially parameter free and gives a reasonable performance.

Figure 6 shows confusion matrices for the two best descriptors. As can be seen, most of the errors are due to mixing up the classes "jogging" and "walking" and mixing up the activities "boxing" and "handclapping", respectively. It is easy to explain why these types of misclassifications occur, since the activities "jogging/running" and "boxing/handclapping" contain similar types of local space-time events. For some of the subjects that were jogging and running in the video sequences, there is a somewhat fuzzy boundary between these two types of activities. If we merge "jogging" and "running" into a single class, the best overall recognition rate on this database increases from 96.4 % (position dependent histograms of optic flow) to 98.4 % (position dependent histograms of spatio-temporal gradients).

To conclude, these results show that it is possible to perform spatio-temporal recognition based on local space-time features. Moreover, considering that all these results have been computed using greedy matching of local image descriptors, there is potential for improvement by including spatio-temporal consistency constraints as well as overall motion descriptors into the recognition scheme.

6   Summary and Discussion

We have presented a set of image descriptors for representing local space-time image structures as well as a method for matching and recognizing spatio-temporal events and activities based on local space-time interest points.

By evaluating the proposed image descriptors on a video database with humans performing different types of actions, we have demonstrated that it is possible to obtain reasonably high recognition rates based on local space-time features. Specifically, we have shown that for this database two novel types of descriptors in terms of local position dependent histograms of either spatio-temporal gradients or optic flow give significantly better results than more traditional approaches of using global histograms, N-jets or principal component analysis of either optic flow or spatio-temporal gradients.

In on-going work, we are planning to extend the proposed histogram-based image descriptors to non-separable histograms as well as to evaluate Mahalanobis distances for matching. We will also perform evaluations on a larger database, including situations with multiple moving objects and cluttered backgrounds. Early results of recognizing human actions in scenes with complex and non-stationary backgrounds have been recently obtained and will be reported elsewhere. In this context, the locality of space-time features and of the proposed image descriptors is of key importance since it allows for matching of corresponding events in scenes with complex backgrounds as illustrated in figure 3.

Concerning other extensions, there is also potential for improving the current greedy point matching procedure to matching schemes which take the internal consistency of matching field as well as the overall motion patterns in the training data more explicitly into account. The replacement of the current nearest-neighbor classification scheme with the SVM classifier has recently been done in [23] and has shown additional increase in recognition performance.

References

1. M.J. Black and A.D. Jepson. Eigentracking: Robust matching and tracking of articulated objects using view-based representation. *IJCV*, 26(1):63–84, 1998.
2. A.F. Bobick and J.W. Davis. The recognition of human movement using temporal templates. *IEEE-PAMI*, 23(3):257–267, 2001.
3. O. Chomat, J. Martin, and J.L. Crowley. A probabilistic sensor for the perception and recognition of activities. In *Proc. ECCV*, volume 1842 of *LNCS*, pages I:487–503. Springer, 2000.
4. A.A. Efros, A.C. Berg, G. Mori, and J. Malik. Recognizing action at a distance. In *Proc. ICCV*, pages 726–733, 2003.
5. R. Fablet and P. Bouthemy. Motion recognition using nonparametric image motion models estimated from temporal and multiscale co-occurrence statistics. *IEEE-PAMI*, 25(12):1619–1624, December 2003.
6. R. Fergus, P. Perona, and A. Zisserman. Object class recognition by unsupervised scale-invariant learning. In *CVPR*, pages 264–271, Madison, Wisconsin, 2003.
7. D. M. Gavrila. The visual analysis of human movement: A survey. *Computer Vision and Image Understanding*, 73(1):82–98, 1999.
8. J. Hoey and J.J. Little. Representation and recognition of complex human motion. In *Proc. CVPR*, pages I:752–759, 2000.
9. Y. Ke and R. Sukthankar. PCA-SIFT: A more disctinctive representation for local image descriptors. Technical Report IRP–TR–03–15, Intel, 2003.
10. J. J. Koenderink and A. J. van Doorn. Representation of local geometry in the visual system. *Biol. Cyb.*, 55:367–375, 1987.
11. I. Laptev and T. Lindeberg. Space-time interest points. In *Proc. ICCV*, pages 432–439, 2003.
12. I. Laptev and T. Lindeberg. Velocity adaptation of space-time interest points. In *Proc. of ICPR, to appear*, 2004.
13. I. Laptev and T. Lindeberg. Velocity-adapted spatio-temporal receptive fields for direct recognition of activities. *IVC*, 22(2):105–116, 2004.
14. T. Lindeberg. Feature detection with automatic scale selection. *IJCV*, 30(2):77–116, 1998.
15. T. Lindeberg. Time-recursive velocity-adapted spatio-temporal scale-space filters. In *Proc. ECCV*, volume 2350 of *LNCS*, pages I:52–67. Springer, 2002.
16. T. Lindeberg and J. Gårding. Shape-adapted smoothing in estimation of 3-D depth cues from affine distortions of local 2-D structure. *IVC*, 15:415–434, 1997.
17. D.G. Lowe. Object recognition from local scale-invariant features. In *Proc. 7th Int. Conf. on Computer Vision*, pages 1150–1157, Corfu, Greece, 1999.
18. B. D. Lukas and T. Kanade. An iterative image registration technique with an application to stereo vision. In *Image Understanding Workshop*, 1981.
19. K. Mikolajczyk and C. Schmid. An affine invariant interest point detector. In *Proc. ECCV*, volume 2350 of *LNCS*, pages I:128–142. Springer, 2002.
20. K. Mikolajczyk and C. Schmid. A performance evaluation of local descriptors. In *Proc. CVPR*, pages II: 257–263, 2003.

21. H.H. Nagel and A. Gehrke. Spatiotemporal adaptive filtering for estimation and segmentation of optical flow fields. In *ECCV'98*, pages 86–102, Freiburg, Germany, June 1998. Springer-Verlag.
22. B. Schiele and J. Crowley. Recognition without correspondence using multidimensional receptive field histograms. *IJCV*, 36(1):31–50, 2000.
23. C. Schüldt, I. Laptev, and B. Caputo. Recognizing human actions: a local SVM approach. In *Proc. of ICPR, to appear*, 2004.
24. M. Shah and R. Jain, editors. *Motion-Based Recognition*. Kluwer, 1997.
25. Y. Yacoob and M. J. Black. Parameterized modeling and recognition of activities. *Computer Vision and Image Understanding*, 73(2):232–247, 1999.
26. L. Zelnik-Manor and M. Irani. Event-based analysis of video. In *Proc. CVPR*, pages II:123–130, 2001.

A Generative Model of
Dense Optical Flow in Layers

Anitha Kannan[1], Brendan Frey[1], and Nebojsa Jojic[2]

[1] Probabilistic and Statistical Inference Group,
University of Toronto, Canada
www.psi.utoronto.ca
{frey, anitha}@psi.utoronto.ca
[2] Microsoft Research, Redmond, USA
jojic@microsoft.com

Abstract. We introduce a generative model of dense flow fields within a layered representation of 3-dimensional scenes. Using probabilistic inference and learning techniques (namely, variational methods), we solve the inverse problem and locally segment the foreground from the background, estimate the nonuniform motion of each, and fill in the disocclusions. To illustrate the usefulness of both the representation and the estimation algorithm, we show results on stabilization and frame interpolation that are obtained by generating from the trained models.

1 Introduction

Traditional methods (c.f. [2]) for estimating optical flow assume brightness constancy across frames and a spatially smooth image motion. These methods can be at a disadvantage in a scene with motion discontinuties which arise when multiple objects are move at different velocities. Motion boundaries carry useful information about the objects in the scene, and in fact, when motion boundaries are estimated correctly, a more reliable flow field can be obtained.

We take a generative model approach for estimating dense flow fields of objects within a layered framework. The model assumes that the scene is a composition of objects from multiple layers (for clarity, we present the case with 2 layers- foreground and background), with objects in each layer undergoing a non-uniform motion. The work we present here assumes that the motion is translational, though it is very straight forward to extend to the case of other transformations. The estimation of the flow field and the appearances and alpha masks are done iteratively, using Expectation Maximization, with guaranteed convergence to locally optimal solution.

2 Related Work

An approach to multiple motion problem views layers as components in a mixture model set-up and provides a soft assignment of pixels to layers (or components) [1, 5]. However, these methods do not model the motion boundaries. The

W.J. MacLean (Ed.): SCVMA 2004, LNCS 3667, pp. 104–114, 2006.

approach taken by Wang & Adelson [10] computes motion vectors at each pixel separately [8] and then regularize the motion fields.

In [6], Jojic & Frey take a generative model approach to jointly infer the uniform motion vector and the appearances and the alpha maps for the objects in different layers. The work of Tao et.al. [9] explicitly models depth ordering of layers and occlusion, along with parameterized motion for the foreground.

Black and Fleet [3] modelled the motion discontinuities directly. In their work, the foreground and background are separated by a straight edge within a single, fixed window in the image sequence. The image sequence within the window is modelled by a generative model that predicts the image at time t from the image at time $t-1$, using unknown state variables that describe the location of the edge and the motions of the foreground and background. They use particle filtering to infer the location of the edge, a motion vector for the foreground and a motion vector for the background at each time step.

In contrast, our model [7] explains the entire image and allows the boundary between background and foreground to have any shape. In fact, the model uses a real-valued map to separate foreground from background, so it is capable of modelling semi-transparent patches of objects. The model operates across multiple frames, allowing local patches that are temporarily occluded to be used to fill in "disocclusions" in later frames.

Our work is closely related to and generalizes the work of [6]. Instead of assuming that object within a layer is moving with a uniform motion, we infer a dense flow field, a motion vector for each pixel, and at the same time learning the segmentation and appearances of objects in different layers.

We present an expectation maximization algorithm for inferring background and foreground motion vectors at every pixel at each time step and at the same time estimating the boundary between the foreground and background.

3   Generative Model

Fig. 1 illustrates our generative model. For each image in the video sequence, our technique estimates an appearance map for the foreground, a transparency map for the foreground, and an appearance map for the background. These maps are estimated from nearby video frames in such a way that every $K \times K$ patch in nearby video frames can be explained by combining a patch from the foreground map with a patch from the background map, using a patch from the transparency map. Here, we show how a fixed patch in 3 video frames is explained by composing patches from the estimated maps.

4   Model of Partially Occluded Patches in Motion

Each video frame in turn is considered as a "reference frame". The appearance maps and the transparency map together with the motion fields for foreground and background are estimated using nearby frames. More generally, the maps and motion fields are coupled by a dynamic model. For example, if the maps and

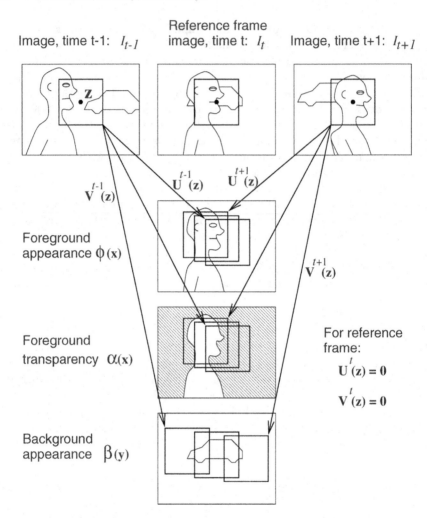

Fig. 1. Nearby video frames are modelled with respect to a reference frame. The appearance of every $K \times K$ patch in nearby frames is modelled using a patch from a foreground transparency map to combine a patch from a foreground appearance map with a patch from a background appearance map. Here, we show how a patch centered at $\mathbf{z}$ in 3 frames is explained by composing displaced patches from the maps. At time $t-1$, the foreground patch and transparency patch displaced by the motion vector $\mathbf{U}^{t-1}(\mathbf{z})$, while the background patch is displaced by the motion vector $\mathbf{V}^{t-1}(\mathbf{z})$. The maps are estimated using the EM algorithm.

motion fields are described by a linear dynamic system, the inference and estimation algorithms presented in later sections are extended to include a Kalman filtering step. For clarity, we focus on estimating the maps and motion fields for a single reference frame.

Let I^t be an $M \times N$ image at time t with pixel intensity $I^t(\mathbf{z})$ at coordinate $\mathbf{z}$. For notational ease, $\mathbf{z}$ is used exclusively as the coordinate in the observed images and $\mathbf{x}$ in the foreground map and the transparency map and $\mathbf{y}$ as the coordinate in the background model.

ϕ is the foreground appearance map and $\phi(\mathbf{x})$ is the foreground appearance at $\mathbf{x}$. α is the transparency map and $\alpha(\mathbf{x})$ is the transparency value in $[0, 1]$ at $\mathbf{x}$. $\alpha(\mathbf{x}) = 1$ indicates the point belongs to the foreground, whereas $\alpha(\mathbf{x}) = 0$ indicates the point belongs to the background. Intermediate values correspond to varying degrees of transparency. β is the background and $\beta(\mathbf{y})$ is the background appearance at $\mathbf{y}$.

In this paper, we use a discrete coordinate system for clarity, although we can easily extend to the case of sub-pixel inference and multi-scale search. To determine the maps and the motion fields, we consider $K \times K$ patches which are translated and compared with patches in nearby frames. We can easily extend to the case where the patches undergo a general affine transformation before comparison with patches in nearby frames. Also, For computational efficiency, we consider motions whereby a patch moves by at most D pixels. However, recent work of Darabiha et.al. [4] has shown that implementation of vision algorithms on FPGAs can lead to real-time performance.

The sequence of images is the only observation to the model. We require to estimate the appearance and transparency maps and the motion fields, all of them depending on each other for reliable estimation. We treat the appearances and the transparency map as the parameters to the model, and encode the uncertainty in the motion vectors due to initial unreliable parameters of the model by treating motion vectors as random variables.

For pixel $I^t(\mathbf{z})$ in the observed image at time t, the foreground and background motion vectors are represented by random variables $\mathbf{U}^t(\mathbf{z})$ and $\mathbf{V}^t(\mathbf{z})$, respectively. The observed patch at $\mathbf{z}$ is composed from a foreground patch centered at $\mathbf{z} + \mathbf{U}^t(\mathbf{z})$, and a background patch centered at $\mathbf{z} + \mathbf{V}^t(\mathbf{z})$, through the transparency map centered at $\mathbf{z} + \mathbf{U}^t(\mathbf{z})$. Since the motion is limited to D pixels, each of these vectors can take on roughly $(2D)^2$ values.

Each $M \times N$ observed frame is decomposed into an $(M - K + 1) \times (N - K + 1)$ grid of $K \times K$ overlapping patches. $\mathcal{P}(\mathbf{z})$ denotes the set of coordinates centered at $\mathbf{z}$.

$$\mathcal{P}(\mathbf{z}) = \{\mathbf{w} : |\mathbf{w} - \mathbf{z}| \leq K\}, \tag{1}$$

and $I(\mathcal{P}(\mathbf{z}))$ denotes the set of observed pixel intensities in the patch centered at $\mathbf{z}$.

Given the foreground appearance map, the transparency map and the background appearance map, the patch appearances are assumed to be independent. While this is clearly not true for any sensible interpretation of the maps, this assumption simplifies the model. For patch $\mathcal{P}(\mathbf{z})$ at time t, the observation likelihood for the corresponding motion vectors is

$$P(I^t(\mathcal{P}(\mathbf{z})) \mid \mathbf{U}^t(\mathbf{z}) = \mathbf{u}, \mathbf{V}^t(\mathbf{z}) = \mathbf{v}) \propto \exp\left[-\sum_{\mathbf{w} \in \mathcal{P}(\mathbf{z})} \right.$$
$$\left. \frac{(\alpha(\mathbf{w}+\mathbf{u})\phi(\mathbf{w}+\mathbf{u})+\bar{\alpha}(\mathbf{w}+\mathbf{u})\beta(\mathbf{w}+\mathbf{v})-I^t(\mathbf{w}))^2}{2\sigma^2}\right] \tag{2}$$

where σ^2 is the variance of the sensor noise, and $\bar{\alpha}(\mathbf{x}) = 1 - \alpha(\mathbf{x})$ is the inverse transparency map. Under this likelihood function, each observed pixel is equal to a composition of a foreground pixel and a background pixel, plus Gaussian sensor noise. σ^2 may be estimated from the frames or set to a small value.

In this work, we assume the motion vectors are independent and uniform *a priori*. Smaller motions can be favored using, *e.g.*, a Gaussian prior on displacement. The foreground and background motion fields can be separately smoothed using independent random process priors.

The joint distribution over the motion fields in all nearby frames $\mathcal{U}$ and $\mathcal{V}$ and the observed patches in all nearby frames $\mathcal{I}$ is

$$
\begin{aligned}
P(\mathcal{U}, \mathcal{V}, \mathcal{I}) &\propto \prod_t \prod_{\mathbf{z}} P(I^t(\mathcal{P}(\mathbf{z})) | \mathbf{U}^t(\mathbf{z}) = \mathbf{u}, \mathbf{V}^t(\mathbf{z}) = \mathbf{v}) \\
&= \prod_t \prod_{\mathbf{z}} \exp\left[- \sum_{\mathbf{w} \in \mathcal{P}(\mathbf{z})} \frac{(\alpha(\mathbf{w}+\mathbf{u})\phi(\mathbf{w}+\mathbf{u}) + \bar{\alpha}(\mathbf{w}+\mathbf{u})\beta(\mathbf{w}+\mathbf{v}) - I^t(\mathbf{w}))^2}{2\sigma^2} \right] \\
&= \exp\left[- \sum_t \sum_{\mathbf{z}} \sum_{\mathbf{w} \in \mathcal{P}(\mathbf{z})} \frac{(\alpha(\mathbf{w}+\mathbf{u})\phi(\mathbf{w}+\mathbf{u}) + \bar{\alpha}(\mathbf{w}+\mathbf{u})\beta(\mathbf{w}+\mathbf{v}) - I^t(\mathbf{w}))^2}{2\sigma^2} \right].
\end{aligned}
$$
$$(3)$$

Given a video sequence, the computational task is to jointly infer the posterior distribution over the motion fields $P(\mathbf{U}^t(\mathbf{z}), \mathbf{V}^t(\mathbf{z}) | I^t)$ of nearby frames, and estimate the model parameters ϕ, α and β. For this, we use the expectation maximization algorithm, wherein we alternate between inferring the distribution over plausible motion fields in the expectation step, and estimating the maps in the maximization step. The resulting procedure guarantees convergence to local optimal solution.

5   Motion Analysis Using the EM Algorithm

Initially, the foreground appearance map ϕ and the background appearance map β are unknown. We set them to the average value of the nearby frames and set the transparency map values to 0.5. Starting from the initial maps, the estimation algorithm alternates between inferring the distribution over motion fields in E-step and estimating the maps in the M-step as described below.

E-Step

In the E-Step, for each image I^t, the posterior distribution $P(\mathbf{U}^t(\mathbf{z}), \mathbf{V}^t(\mathbf{z}) | I^t)$ over the the foreground motion vector $\mathbf{U}^t(\mathbf{z})$ and the background motion vector $\mathbf{V}^t(\mathbf{z})$ is computed for each coordinate $\mathbf{z}$ in the observed image.

This posterior is computed by examining all possible ways in which the patch centered at $\mathbf{z}$ in I^t can be composed by displacing patches from the foreground and background maps. The posterior distribution is

$$P(\mathbf{U}^t(\mathbf{z}) = \mathbf{u}, \mathbf{V}^t(\mathbf{z}) = \mathbf{v} | I^t) = \rho \exp\left[- \sum_{\mathbf{w} \in \mathcal{P}(\mathbf{z})} \right.$$

$$\left. \frac{(\alpha(\mathbf{w}+\mathbf{u})\phi(\mathbf{w}+\mathbf{u}) + \bar{\alpha}(\mathbf{w}+\mathbf{u})\beta(\mathbf{w}+\mathbf{v}) - I^t(\mathbf{w}))^2}{2\sigma^2} \right], \tag{4}$$

where ρ ensures that $\sum_{\mathbf{u}} \sum_{\mathbf{v}} P(\mathbf{U}^t(\mathbf{z}) = \mathbf{u}, \mathbf{V}^t(\mathbf{z}) = \mathbf{v} | I^t) = 1$.

M-Step

The set of all coordinates whose $K \times K$ patches can "reach" coordinate $\mathbf{x}$ when moved by at most D is

$$\mathcal{R}(\mathbf{x}) = \{\mathbf{z} : |\mathbf{x} - \mathbf{z}| \leq (K - 1)/2 + D\}. \tag{5}$$

The set of all motion vectors for the patch at $\mathbf{z}$ that cause a pixel in the patch to be mapped to $\mathbf{x}$ is

$$\mathcal{M}(\mathbf{x}, \mathbf{z}) = \{\mathbf{u} : |(\mathbf{x} - \mathbf{z}) - \mathbf{u}| \leq (K - 1)/2; |\mathbf{u}| \leq D\}. \tag{6}$$

Define,

$$\left\langle \aleph \right\rangle = \sum_t \sum_{\mathbf{z} \in \mathcal{R}(\mathbf{x})} \sum_{\mathbf{u} \in \mathcal{M}(\mathbf{x}, \mathbf{z})} \sum_{\mathbf{v} \in \mathcal{M}(\mathbf{x}, \mathbf{z})} P(\mathbf{U}^t(\mathbf{z}) = \mathbf{u}, \mathbf{V}^t(\mathbf{z}) = \mathbf{v} | I^t) \aleph$$

After computing $P(\mathbf{U}^t(\mathbf{z}) = \mathbf{u}, \mathbf{V}^t(\mathbf{z}) = \mathbf{v} | I^t)$ for all t in the E-Step, the foreground appearance is modified:

$$\phi(\mathbf{x}) \leftarrow \left(\left\langle \alpha(\mathbf{x})^2 \right\rangle \right)^{-1} \cdot \left(\left\langle \alpha(\mathbf{x})(I^t(\mathbf{x} - \mathbf{u}) - \bar{\alpha}(\mathbf{x})\beta(\mathbf{x} - \mathbf{u} + \mathbf{v})) \right\rangle \right) \tag{7}$$

Next, the transparency map is modified, using the foreground appearance map modified above:

$$\alpha(\mathbf{x}) \leftarrow \left(\left\langle \left(\phi(\mathbf{x}) - \beta(\mathbf{x} - \mathbf{u} + \mathbf{v}) \right)^2 \right\rangle \right)^{-1}$$

$$\cdot \left(\left\langle (\phi(\mathbf{x}) - \beta(\mathbf{x} - \mathbf{u} + \mathbf{v}))(I^t(\mathbf{x} - \mathbf{u}) - \beta(\mathbf{x} - \mathbf{u} + \mathbf{v})) \right\rangle \right) \tag{8}$$

In fact, before modifying the transparency map, an E-Step can be used to recompute the posterior, which changes once the foreground appearance is modified. Although this step is not required to guarantee convergence, we find it speeds up convergence. Next, the background appearance is modified:

$$\beta(\mathbf{y}) \leftarrow \left(\left\langle \bar{\alpha}(\mathbf{y} - \mathbf{v} + \mathbf{u})^2 \right\rangle \right)^{-1}$$

$$\cdot \left(\left\langle \bar{\alpha}(\mathbf{y} - \mathbf{v} + \mathbf{u}) \left(I^t(\mathbf{y} - \mathbf{v}) - \alpha(\mathbf{y} - \mathbf{v} + \mathbf{u})\phi(\mathbf{y} - \mathbf{v} + \mathbf{u}) \right) \right\rangle \right). \tag{9}$$

Again, before modifying the background appearance, an E-Step can be applied to update the posterior.

6   Experiments

6.1   Sequence 1

We present results on a sequence of 5 frames, each of size 60×60 in which a person is moving in front of a cluttered background. Fig. 2d & e shows the sequence. We used 7x7 overlapping patches. For computational reasons, we restricted the search space for the foreground motion to be 7 pixels for horizontal shifts, and 2 pixels for vertical shifts. Similarly, for background motion, the search space is

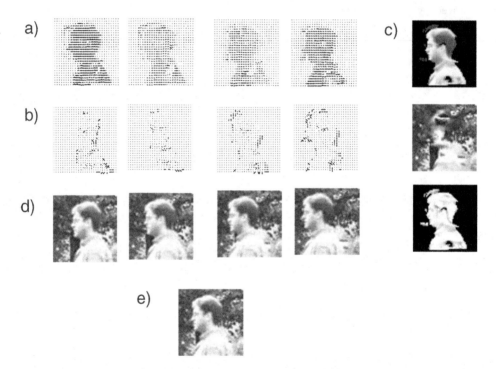

Fig. 2. a) Inferred flow fields for the foreground motion b) Inferred flow fields for the background motion c)the learned parameters of the model - appearance maps and the transparency map. These are inferred using the sequence of 5 frames in d) with e)as the reference frame.

Fig. 3. Five frames obtained from generating from the model

restricted to 1 pixel in either directions. Thus, the posterior over motion field involved a distribution over $75 \times 9 = 675$ values.

On convergence, we can reliably use MAP estimate of the posterior distribution for each pixel as the flow for that pixel since the posterior gets to be peaky. Fig. 2a-b shows the flow fields for both foreground and the background motion for each frame with respect to the reference frame. For ease of viewing, the flow fields for foreground motion is masked using its transparency mask.

Fig. 2c shows the learned appearance maps for the foreground and the background, and the transparency map. We find that the background accounts for pixels that were occluded in some frames. The transparency map is reasonable given that we used only 5 frames to train the model.

We can use the generative model to generate new data, and in particular do frame interpolation. We used the trained model to obtain frames between the reference frame and the first frame in the sequence (Fig. 3).

6.2   Sequence 2: Flower Garden Sequence

The flower garden sequence has a fast moving tree in front of slow moving complex background, recorded using a camera mounted on a moving vehicle. We used a small subset of the sequence consisting of 7 frames. The first and last frames of the sequence we used is in Fig. 4 b & c. We used 15x15 fully overlapping patches. The search space for foreground motion is restricted to lie

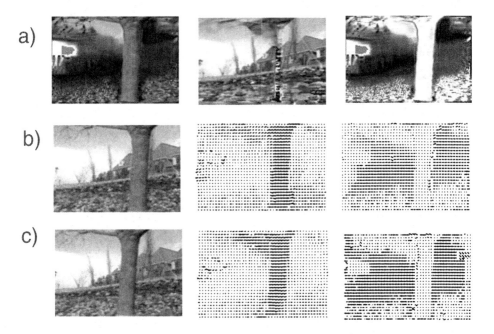

Fig. 4. a) appearance and transparency maps. b) the first frame and its foreground and background motion fields c) last frame and its motion fields.

between -10 and 10 for horizontal motion, and -2 to 2 for vertical motion. For the background motion, the search is between -2 and 2 for horizontal shifts and -1 and 1 for vertical shifts. Thus, the posterior distribution assigns probability for each of the 1575 flow combinations.

Fig. 4a shows the foreground (masked by mask) and background appearances and the transparency map. The portion of garden closer to observer is assigned to

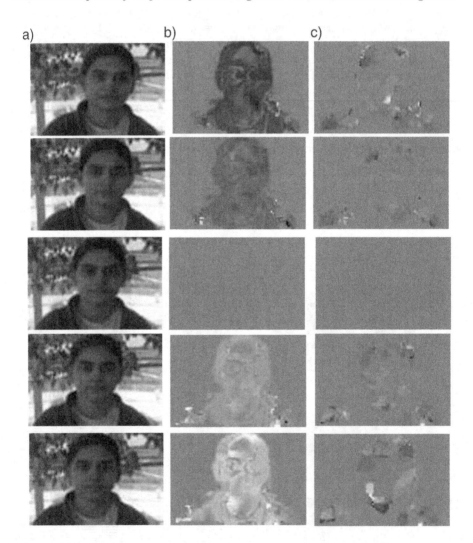

Fig. 5. a) Five (alternate) frames from the sequence, with the reference frame in the middle b) horizontal component and c) vertical component of foreground motion. Pixels for motion are scaled such that white is 9 pixels shift to right (horizontal motion) or up(vertical motion), and black is 9 pixels shift in the opposite direction, with gray representing no motion. We have masked the flow fields with appropriate transparency map for the frame for clarity.

foreground, a possible reason being that the search space for background is very much restricted (within 2 pixel deviation), and the garden closer to the observer moves faster than that. Hence, it uses foreground to explain its motion better.

6.3   Sequence-3

We considered a sequence of 9 frames in which a person turns her hand within plane. Fig. 5a shows five frames from the sequence. We fixed the background to be stationary, and allowed foreground displacement to be between -9 and 9 in both directions. The estimated flow fields for the frames are shown in Fig. 5b-c. The flow fields elucidate the non-uniform motion that the foreground object undergoes. In Fig. 6, we present the parameters learned using the estimation. The model has done a reasonable job of learning the transparency mask even though the data is limited and some of the pixels in the foreground object are stationary. Fig. 7 shows the interpolated sequence of 10 frames obtained by generating from the model.

Fig. 6. The parameters learned using a sequence of 9 frames of a person turning her head, as shown in Fig. 7

Fig. 7. Ten frames generated from the model between the reference frame(shown here as the first frame) and the last frame of the original sequence (shown here as the last frame)

7   Summary and Conclusions

We presented a layered generative model for inferring dense flow fields. Using unsupervised learning and variational method for inference, we solve the problem of estimating the appearances of foreground and background objects by segmenting local patches and inferring its local non uniform motion. This enables filling in of disocclusions. Being a generative model, learned model can be used to generate data and thus readily available for tasks such as frame interpolation.

References

1. Ayer, S. & Sawhney, H   Layered representation of motion video using robust maximum-likelihood estimation of mixture models and MDL encoding In *Proc. IEEE International Conference on Computer Vision*, 1995
2. Barron, J.L., Fleet, D.J., & Beauchemin Performance of optical flow techniques In *International Journal of Computer Vision*, 12(1):4377, 1994.
3. Black, M.J. & Fleet, D.J. Probabilistic detection and tracking of motion discontinuities In *International Journal of Computer Vision*, 36(3):171-193, 2000
4. Darabiha A, Rose JR & MacLean WJ Video Rate Stereo Depth Measurement on Programmable Hardware. In *Proc. of IEEE Conference on CVPR* , 2003
5. Jepson, A. & Black, M.J. Mixture models for optical flow computation In *In Partitioning Data Sets: With Applications to Psychology, Vision and Target Tracking, Ingmer Cox, Pierre Hansen, and Bela Julesz (Eds.), AMS Pub.: Providence, pp. 271 286. RI, DIMACS Workshop*, 1993
6. Jojic, N. & Frey, B.J. Learning flexible sprites in video layers In *Proc. of IEEE Conference on CVPR* ,1999
7. Jojic, N. Frey, B.J. & Kannan,A. A Generative model of dense optical flow in Layers *University of Toronto Technical Report* PSI-2001-11, 2001
8. Lucas, B.D. & Kanade, T., An Iterative Image Registration Technique with an Application to Stereo Vision In *Proceedings of the 7th International Joint Conference on Artificial Intelligence*, 1981
9. Zhou,Y. & Tao,H. A Background Layer Model for Object Tracking through Occlusion In *Proc. IEEE International Conf. on Computer Vision, ICCV*, 2003
10. Wang, J.Y.A. & Adelson, E.H Layered Representation for Motion Analysis In *IEEE Conference on Computer Vision and Pattern Recognition*,1993
11. Weiss, Y. & Adelson, E.H A unified mixture framework for motion segmentation: Incorporating spatial coherence and estimating the number of models In *Proc. IEEE Computer Vision and Pattern Recognition*, 1996.

Analysis and Interpretation of Multiple Motions Through Surface Saliency*

Mircea Nicolescu[1], Changki Min[2], and Gérard Medioni[2]

[1] Department of Computer Science, University of Nevada, Reno
Reno, NV 89557
`mircea@cs.unr.edu`
[2] Integrated Media Systems Center, University of Southern California,
Los Angeles, CA 90089-0273
`{cmin, medioni}@iris.usc.edu`

Abstract. The problem of recovering the 3-D camera and scene structure has been intensively studied and is considered well understood. Starting with two images, a process of establishing point correspondences is usually followed by the estimation of epipolar geometry while also rejecting outlier matches, and finally by 3-D structure estimation. However, most existing methods tend to fail in the combined presence of noise and multiple motions, since no single constraint applies to the entire set of matches. Hence, image registration becomes a more challenging problem, as the matching and registration phases become interdependent. We propose a novel approach that decouples the above operations, allowing for separate handling of matching, outlier rejection, grouping and 3-D interpretation. Our method first determines an accurate representation in terms of dense velocities, segmented motion regions and boundaries, by enforcing only the smoothness of image motion, followed by the extraction of 3-D camera and scene geometry.

1 Introduction

Most existing methods for recovering the camera and 3-D scene structure from a set of correspondences are usually based on the assumption that a single constraint (e.g., rigidity, or the epipolar constraint) can be enforced on the entire set. Given two views of a static scene, a set of matching points – typically corresponding to salient image features – are first obtained by methods such as cross-correlation. Assuming that matches are perfect, a simple Eight Point Algorithm [1] can be used for estimating the fundamental matrix, and thus the epipolar geometry of the cameras is determined. A dense set of matches can be then established, and finally the scene structure is recovered through triangulation. The simplistic approach described above performs reasonably well only when (i) the set of matches contains no outlier noise, and (ii) the scene is rigid – i.e., without objects having independent motions.

---

* This research has been funded in part by the Integrated Media Systems Center, an NSF Engineering Research Center, Cooperative Agreement No. EEC-9529152, and by NSF Grant 9811883.

W. J. MacLean (Ed.): SCVMA 2004, LNCS 3667, pp. 115–126, 2006.

The first assumption almost never holds, since image measurements are bound to be imperfect, and matching techniques will never produce accurate correspondences, mainly due to occlusion or lack of texture. In the presence of incorrect matches, linear methods are very likely to fail. The problem can be reliably solved by robust methods, which involve non-linear optimization [2][3], and normalization of data before fundamental matrix estimation [4].

However, if the second assumption is also violated by the presence of multiple independent motions, even the robust methods may become unstable, as the scene no longer corresponds to a rigid configuration. Even if the dominant epipolar geometry is recovered (for example, the one corresponding to the static background), it is not very clear how to handle misfits – they may be caused by outlier noise, independent motions, or even non-rigid motion.

The core inadequacy of most existing methods is that they attempt to enforce a global constraint – such as the epipolar one – on a data set which may include, in addition to noise, independent subsets that are subject to separate constraints. In this context, it is indeed very difficult to recover structure from motion and segment the scene into independently moving objects, if these tasks are performed simultaneously.

In order to address these difficulties, we propose a novel approach that decouples the above operations, allowing for explicit and separate handling of matching, outlier rejection, grouping, and recovery of camera and scene structure. In the first step, we determine an accurate representation in terms of dense velocities (equivalent to point correspondences), segmented motion regions and boundaries, by using only the smoothness of image motion [5]. In the second step we proceed with the extraction of scene and camera 3-D geometry, separately on each rigid component of the scene. Note that our approach follows Ullman's interpretation of visual motion [6], in that the correspondence process takes place prior to 3-D interpretation.

The main advantage of our approach is that at the interpretation stage, noisy matches have been already rejected, and matches have been grouped according to the distinct moving objects in the scene. Therefore, standard methods can be reliably applied on each data subset in order to determine the 3-D camera and scene structure.

1.1 Previous Work

Linear methods [1][7][8] can be used for estimation of the fundamental matrix, in the absence of noisy matches or moving objects. The Eight Point Algorithm [1] recovers the essential/fundamental matrix from two calibrated/uncalibrated images, by solving a system of linear equations. A minimum of eight points is needed – if more are available, a least mean square minimization is used. To ensure that the resulting matrix satisfies the rank two requirement, its singularity is usually enforced [4][9].

In order to handle outlier noise, more complex, non-linear iterative optimization methods are proposed [3][10][11]. These techniques use objective functions, such as distance between points and corresponding epipolar lines, or gradient-weighted epipolar errors, to guide the optimization process. Despite their increased robustness, iterative optimization methods in general require somewhat careful initialization for early convergence to the correct optimum. One of the most successful algorithms in this class is LMedS [3], which uses the least median of squares and data sub-sampling to discard outliers by solving a non-linear minimization problem.

RANSAC [12] consists of random sampling of a minimum subset with seven pairs of matching points for parameter estimation. The candidate subset that maximizes the number of inliers and minimizes the residual is the solution. Statistical measures are used to derive the minimum number of sample subsets. Although LMedS and RANSAC are considered to be some of the most robust methods, it is worth noting that these techniques still require a majority of the data to be correct, or else some statistical assumption is needed. If false matches and independent motions exist, these methods may fail or become less attractive, since in the latter case, many matching points on the moving objects are discarded as outliers.

In [13], Pritchett and Zisserman propose the use of local planar homographies, generated by Gaussian pyramid techniques. However, the homography assumption does not generally apply to the entire image.

1.2 Outline of the Approach

The first step of the proposed method formulates the motion analysis problem as an inference of motion layers from a noisy and possibly sparse point set in a 4-D space. In order to compute a dense set of matches (equivalent to a velocity field) and to segment the image into motion regions, we use an approach based on a *layered 4-D representation* of data, and a *voting scheme* for communication. First we establish candidate matches through a multi-scale, normalized cross-correlation procedure. Following a perceptual grouping perspective, each potential match is seen as a token characterized by four attributes – the image coordinates (x, y) in the first image, and the velocity with the components (v_x, v_y).

Tokens are encapsulated as (x, y, v_x, v_y) points in the 4-D space, this being a natural way of expressing the spatial separation of tokens according to *both* velocities and image coordinates. In general, for each pixel (x, y) there can be several candidate velocities, so each 4-D point (x, y, v_x, v_y) represents a potential match.

Within this representation, smoothness of motion is embedded in the concept of surface saliency exhibited by the data. By letting the tokens communicate their mutual affinity through voting, noisy matches are eliminated as they receive little support, and distinct moving regions are extracted as smooth, *salient surface layers* in 4-D.

The second step interprets the image motion by estimating the 3-D scene structure and camera geometry. First a rigidity test is performed on the matches within each object, to identify potential non-rigid (deforming) objects, and also between objects, to merge those that move rigidly together but have separate image motions due to depth discontinuities. Finally, the epipolar geometry is estimated separately for each rigid component by using standard methods for parameter estimation (such as the normalized Eight Point Algorithm, LMedS or RANSAC), and the scene structure and camera motion are recovered by using the dense velocity field.

2 The Voting Framework

2.1 Voting in 2-D

The use of a voting process for feature inference from sparse and noisy data was formalized into a unified tensor framework by Medioni, Lee and Tang [14]. The input data is encoded as tensors, then support information (including proximity and smoothness of continuity) is propagated by voting. The only free parameter is the scale of analysis, which is indeed an inherent property of visual perception.

In the 2-D case, the salient features to be extracted are points and curves. Each token is encoded as a second order symmetric 2-D tensor, geometrically equivalent to an ellipse. It is described by a 2×2 eigensystem, where eigenvectors e_1 and e_2 give the ellipse orientation and eigenvalues λ_1 and λ_2 are the ellipse size. The tensor is represented as a matrix $S = \lambda_1 \cdot e_1 e_1^T + \lambda_2 \cdot e_2 e_2^T$.

An input token that represents a curve element is encoded as a *stick tensor*, where e_2 represents the curve tangent and e_1 the curve normal, while $\lambda_1=1$ and $\lambda_2=0$. A point element is encoded as a *ball tensor*, with no preferred orientation, and $\lambda_1=\lambda_2=1$.

The communication between tokens is performed through a voting process, where each token casts a vote at each site in its neighborhood. The size and shape of this neighborhood, and the vote strength and orientation are encapsulated in predefined voting fields, one for each feature type – there is a stick voting field and a ball voting field in the 2-D case. The fields are generated based only on the scale factor σ. Vote orientation corresponds to the smoothest continuation from voter to recipient, while vote strength $VS(\vec{d})$ decays with distance $|\vec{d}|$ between them, and with curvature ρ:

$$VS(\vec{d}) = e^{-\left(\frac{|\vec{d}|^2+\rho^2}{\sigma^2}\right)} \tag{1}$$

Fig. 1 shows how votes are generated to build the 2-D stick field. A tensor P where curve information is locally known (illustrated by curve normal $\vec{N}_p$) casts a vote at its neighbor Q. The vote orientation is chosen so that it ensures a smooth curve continuation through a circular arc from voter P to recipient Q. To propagate the curve normal $\vec{N}$ thus obtained, the vote $V_{stick}(\vec{d})$ sent from P to Q is encoded as a tensor according to:

$$V_{stick}(\vec{d}) = VS(\vec{d}) \cdot \vec{N}\vec{N}^T \tag{2}$$

Fig. 2 shows the 2-D stick field, with its color-coded strength. When the voter is a ball tensor, with no information known locally, the vote is generated by rotating a stick vote in the 2-D plane and integrating all contributions. The 2-D ball field is shown in Fig. 3.

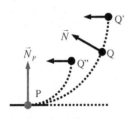

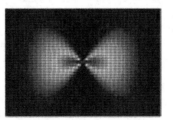

Fig. 1. Vote generation   **Fig. 2.** 2-D stick field   **Fig. 3.** 2-D ball field

At each receiving site, the collected votes are combined through simple tensor addition, producing generic 2-D tensors. During voting, tokens that lie on a smooth curve reinforce each other, and the tensors deform according to the prevailing orientation. Each tensor encodes the local orientation of geometric features (given by the tensor orientation), and their saliency (given by the tensor shape and size). For a generic 2-D tensor, its curve saliency is given by $(\lambda_1-\lambda_2)$, the curve normal orientation by e_1, while its point saliency is given by λ_2. Therefore, the voting process infers curves and junctions simultaneously, while also identifying outlier noise.

2.2   Extension to 4-D

Table 1 shows all the geometric features that appear in a 4-D space and their representation as *elementary* 4-D tensors, where n and t represent normal and tangent vectors, respectively. Note that a surface in the 4-D space can be characterized by two normal vectors, or by two tangent vectors. From a *generic* 4-D tensor that results after voting, the geometric features are extracted as shown in Table 2.

The 4-D voting fields are obtained as follows. First the 4-D stick field is generated in a similar manner to the 2-D stick field (see Fig. 1). Then, the other three voting fields are built by integrating all the contributions obtained by rotating a 4-D stick field around appropriate axes. In particular, the 4-D ball field – the only one directly used here – is generated according to:

$$V_{ball}(\vec{d}) = \int\limits_{0}^{2\pi}\int\int R\,V_{stick}(R^{-1}\vec{d})\,R^T\,d\theta_{xy}d\theta_{xu}d\theta_{xv} \qquad (3)$$

where x, y, u, v are the 4-D coordinates axes and R is the rotation matrix with angles θ_{xy}, θ_{xu}, θ_{xv}.

Table 1. Elementary tensors in 4-D

Feature	$\lambda_1\ \lambda_2\ \lambda_3\ \lambda_4$	$e_1\ e_2\ e_3\ e_4$	Tensor
point	1 1 1 1	Any orthonormal basis	Ball
curve	1 1 1 0	$n_1\ n_2\ n_3\ t$	C-Plate
surface	1 1 0 0	$n_1\ n_2\ t_1\ t_2$	S-Plate
volume	1 0 0 0	$n\ \ t_1\ \ t_2\ \ t_3$	Stick

Table 2. A generic tensor in 4-D

Feature	Saliency	Normals	Tangents
point	λ_4	none	none
curve	$\lambda_3 - \lambda_4$	$e_1\ e_2\ e_3$	e_4
surface	$\lambda_2 - \lambda_3$	$e_1\ e_2$	$e_3\ e_4$
volume	$\lambda_1 - \lambda_2$	e_1	$e_2\ e_3\ e_4$

The data structure used to store the tensors is an *approximate nearest neighbor (ANN) k-d tree* [15]. The space complexity is $O(n)$, where n is the input size (the total number of candidate tokens). The average time complexity of the voting process is $O(\mu n)$ where μ is the average number of candidate tokens in the neighborhood. Therefore, in contrast to other voting techniques, such as the Hough Transform, both time and space complexities of the Tensor Voting methodology are *independent* of the dimensionality of the desired feature.

3 Motion Segmentation

We take as input two image frames that involve general motion – that is, both the camera and the objects in the scene may be moving. For illustration purposes, we give a description of our approach by using a specific example – the two images in Fig. 4(a) are taken with a handheld moving camera, while the stack of books has been moved between taking the two pictures.

Matching. For every pixel in the first image, the goal at this stage is to produce candidate matches in the second image. We use a normalized cross-correlation procedure [16], where all peaks of correlation are retained as candidates. When a peak is found, its position is also adjusted for sub-pixel precision according to the correlation values of its neighbors. Finally, each candidate match is represented as a (x,y,v_x,v_y) point in the 4-D space of image coordinates and pixel velocities, with respect to the first image.

Since we want to increase the likelihood of including the correct match among the candidates, we repeat this process at multiple scales, by using different correlation window sizes. Small windows have the advantage of capturing fine detail, and are effective close to the motion boundaries, but produce considerable noise in areas lacking texture or having small repetitive patterns. Larger windows generate smoother matches, but their performance degrades in large areas along motion boundaries. We have experimented with a large range of window sizes, and found that best results are obtained by using only two or three different sizes, that should include at least a very small one. In practice we used three correlation windows, with 3x3, 5x5 and 7x7 sizes.

The resulting candidates appear as a cloud of (x,y,v_x,v_y) points in the 4-D space. Fig. 4(b) shows the candidate matches. In order to display 4-D data, the last component of each 4-D point has been dropped – the 3 dimensions shown are x and y (in the horizontal plane), and v_x (the height). The motion layers can be already perceived as their tokens are grouped in two layers surrounded by noisy matches.

Extracting statistically salient structures from such noisy data is very difficult for most existing methods. Because our voting framework is robust to considerable amounts of noise, we can afford using the multiple window sizes in order to extract the motion layers.

Selection. Since no information is initially known, each potential match is encoded into a 4-D *ball tensor*. Then each token casts votes by using the 4-D *ball voting field*. During voting there is strong support between tokens that lie on a smooth surface (layer), while communication between layers is reduced by the spatial separation in the 4-D space of both image coordinates and pixel velocities. For each pixel (x,y) we

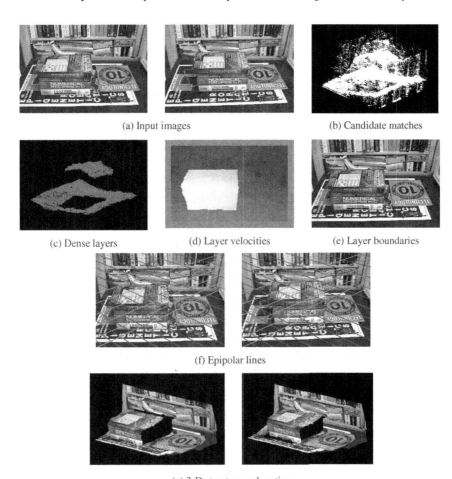

(a) Input images

(b) Candidate matches

(c) Dense layers

(d) Layer velocities

(e) Layer boundaries

(f) Epipolar lines

(g) 3-D structure and motion

Fig. 4. BOOKS sequence

retain the candidate match with the highest surface saliency (λ_2-λ_3), and we reject the others as wrong matches. By voting we also estimate the normals to layers at each token as e_1 and e_2.

Outlier rejection. In the selection step, we kept only the most salient candidate at each pixel. However, there are pixels where all candidates are wrong, such as in areas lacking texture. Therefore now we eliminate all tokens that have received very little support. Typically we reject all tokens with surface saliency less that 10% of the average saliency of the entire set.

Densification. Since the previous step created holes (i.e., pixels where no velocity is available), we must infer them from the neighbors by using a smoothness constraint. For each pixel (x, y) without an assigned velocity we try to find the best (v_x, v_y) location at which to place a newly generated token. The candidates considered are all the discrete points (v_x, v_y) between the minimum and maximum velocities in the set, within a neighborhood of the (x,y) point. At each candidate position (x,y,v_x,v_y) we accumulate votes, according to the same Tensor Voting framework that we have used so far. After voting, the candidate token with maximal surface saliency $(\lambda_2-\lambda_3)$ is retained, and its (v_x,v_y) coordinate represent the most likely velocity at (x,y). By following this procedure at every (x,y) image location we generate a *dense velocity field*. Note that in this process, along with velocities we simultaneously infer layer orientations. A 3-D view of the dense layers is shown in Fig. 4(c).

Segmentation. The next step is to group tokens into *regions*, by using again the smoothness constraint. We start from an arbitrary point in the image, assign a region label to it, and try to recursively propagate this label to all its image neighbors. In order to decide whether the label must be propagated, we use the smoothness of both velocity and layer orientation as a grouping criterion. Fig. 4(d) illustrates the recovered v_x velocities within layers (dark corresponds to low velocity).

Boundary inference. The extracted layers may still be over or under-extended along the true object boundaries. This situation typically occurs in areas subject to occlusion, where the initial correlation procedure may generate wrong matches that are consistent with the correct ones, and therefore could not be rejected as outlier noise. The boundaries of the extracted layers give us a good estimate for the position and overall orientation of the true boundaries. We combine this knowledge with monocular cues (intensity edges) from the original images in order to build a boundary saliency map within the uncertainty zone along the layers margins. At each location in this area, a 2-D stick tensor is generated, having an orientation normal to the image gradient, and a saliency proportional to the gradient magnitude.

The smoothness and continuity of the boundary is then enforced through a 2-D voting process, and the true boundary is extracted as the most salient curve within the saliency map. Finally, pixels from the uncertainty zone are reassigned to regions according to the new boundaries, and their velocities are recomputed. Fig. 4(e) shows the refined motion boundaries, that indeed correspond to the actual object.

4   Interpretation of Image Motion

So far we have not made any assumption regarding the 3-D motion, and the only constraint used has been the smoothness of image motion. The observed image motion could have been produced by the 3-D motion of objects in the scene, or the camera motion, or both. Furthermore, some of the objects may suffer non-rigid motion.

For classification we used an algorithm introduced by McReynolds and Lowe [17], that verifies the potential rigidity of a set of minimum six point correspondences from two views under perspective projection. The rigidity test is performed on a subset of matches within each object, to identify potential non-rigid objects, and also across objects, to merge those that move rigidly together but have distinct image motions due to depth discontinuities. It is also worth mentioning that the rigidity test is actually able to only guarantee the *non-rigidity* of a given configuration. Indeed, if the rigidity test fails, it means that the image motion is not compatible to a rigid 3-D motion, and therefore the configuration *must* be non-rigid. If the test succeeds, it only asserts that a possible rigid 3-D motion *exists*, that is compatible to the given image motion. However, this computational approach corresponds to the way human vision operates – as shown in [6], human perception solves this inherent ambiguity by always choosing a rigid interpretation when possible.

The remaining task at this stage is to determine the object (or camera) motion, and the scene structure. Since wrong matches have been eliminated, and correct matches are already grouped according to the rigidly moving objects in the scene, standard methods for reconstruction can be reliably applied. For increased robustness, we chose to use RANSAC [12] to recover the epipolar geometry for each rigid object, followed by an estimation of camera motion and projective scene structure.

The following discussion describes each case, illustrated with experimental results.

Multiple rigid motions. This case is illustrated by the BOOKS example in Fig. 4, where two sets of matches have been detected, corresponding to the two distinct objects – the stack of books and the background. The rigidity test shows that, while each object moves rigidly, they cannot be merged into a single rigid structure. The recovered epipolar geometry is illustrated in Fig. 4(f), while the 3-D scene structure and motion are shown in Fig. 4(g).

The CYLINDERS example, shown in Fig. 5, is adapted from Ullman [6], and consists of two images of random points in a sparse configuration, taken from the surfaces of two transparent co-axial cylinders, rotating in opposite directions. This extremely difficult example clearly illustrates the power of our approach, which is able to determine accurate point correspondences and scene structure – even from a sparse input, based on motion cues only (without any monocular cues), and for transparent motion.

Single rigid motion. This is the stereo case, illustrated by the CANDY BOX example in Fig. 6, where the scene is static and the camera is moving. Due to the depth disparity between the box and the background, their image motions do not satisfy the

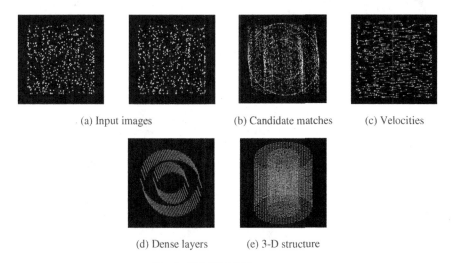

(a) Input images   (b) Candidate matches   (c) Velocities

(d) Dense layers   (e) 3-D structure

Fig. 5. CYLINDERS sequence

smoothness constraint together, and thus they have been segmented as two separate objects. However, the rigidity test shows that the two objects form a rigid configuration, and therefore are labeled as a single object. The epipolar geometry estimation and scene reconstruction are then performed on the entire set of matches. Along with the 3-D structure, Fig. 6(g) also shows the two recovered camera positions.

Non-rigid motion. The FLAG example, shown in Fig. 7, is a synthetic sequence where sparse random dots from the surface of a waving flag are displayed in two frames. The configuration is recognized as non-rigid, and therefore no reconstruction is attempted. However, since the *image motion* is smooth, our framework is still able to determine correct correspondences, extract motion layers, segment non-rigid objects, and label them as such.

We also analyzed a standard sequence (the TEDDY example – Fig. 8) with ground truth available, to provide a quantitative estimate for the performance of our approach, as compared to other methods. As shown in Table 3 (partially reproduced

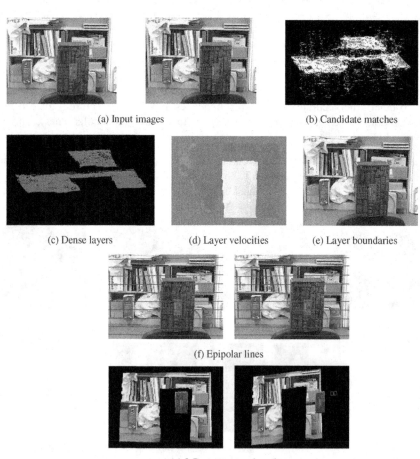

(a) Input images   (b) Candidate matches

(c) Dense layers   (d) Layer velocities   (e) Layer boundaries

(f) Epipolar lines

(g) 3-D structure and motion

Fig. 6. CANDY BOX sequence

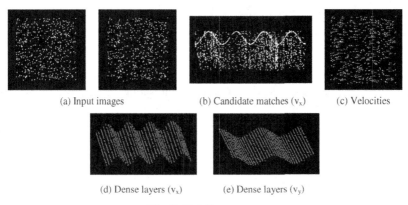

(a) Input images   (b) Candidate matches (v_x)   (c) Velocities

(d) Dense layers (v_x)   (e) Dense layers (v_y)

Fig. 7. FLAG sequence

(a) An input image   (b) Ground truth disparity map   (c) Tensor Voting disparity map

Fig. 8. TEDDY sequence

Table 3. TEDDY sequence – results [18]

Methods	Error Rate
Tensor Voting	**15.4%**
Sum of Squared Differences	26.5%
Dynamic Programming	30.1%
Graph Cuts	29.3%

from [18]), our voting-based approach has the smallest error rate (percentage of pixels with a disparity error greater than 1), among the techniques mentioned.

5 Conclusions

We have presented a novel approach that decouples grouping and interpretation of visual motion, allowing for explicit and separate handling of matching, outlier rejection, grouping, and recovery of camera and scene structure. The proposed framework is able to handle data sets containing large amounts of outlier noise, as well as multiple independently moving objects, or non-rigid objects.

Our methodology for extracting motion layers is based on a *layered 4-D representation* of data, and a *voting scheme* for token communication. It allows for structure inference without using any prior knowledge of the motion model, based on the smoothness of motion only, while consistently handling both smooth moving regions and motion discontinuities. The method is also computationally robust, being non-iterative, and does not depend on critical thresholds, the only free parameter being the scale of analysis.

We plan to extend our approach by incorporating information from multiple frames, and to study the possibility of using an adaptive scale of analysis in the voting process.

References

[1]   H. C. Longuet-Higgins, "A Computer Algorithm for Reconstructing a Scene from Two Projections", Nature, 293:133-135, 1981.

[2]   Adam, E. Rivlin, L. Shimshoni, "Ror: Rejection of Outliers by Rotations", Trans. PAMI, 23(1), pp. 78-84, 2001.

[3]   Z. Zhang, "Determining the Epipolar Geometry and Its Uncertainty: A Review", IJCV, 27(2), pp. 161-195, 1998.

[4]   R. I. Hartley, "In Defense of the 8-Point Algorithm", PAMI, 19(6), pp. 580-593, 1997.

[5]   M. Nicolescu, G. Medioni, "Layered 4D Representation and Voting for Grouping from Motion", Trans. PAMI – Special Issue on Perceptual Organization in Computer Vision, vol. 25, no. 4, pp. 492-501, 2003.

[6]   S. Ullman, "The Interpretation of Visual Motion", MIT Press, 1979.

[7]   T. Huang and A. Netravali, "Motion and Structure from Feature Correspondences: A Review", P-IEEE, vol. 82, pp. 252-268, 1994.

[8]   R. Hartley, "Projective Reconstruction and Invariants from Multiple Images", Trans. PAMI, vol. 16, no. 10, pp. 1036-1040, 1994.

[9]   O. Faugeras, "Stratification of 3-D Vision: Projective, Affine, and Metric Representations", J. Optical Society of America, 12(3), pp. 465-484, 1995.

[10] Q.-T. Luong, O. Faugeras, "The Fundamental Matrix: Theory, Algorithms, and Stability Analysis", IJCV, vol. 17, pp. 43-76, 1996.

[11] R. Mohr, F. Veillon, L. Quan, "Relative 3D Reconstruction Using Multiple Uncalibrated Images", CVPR, pp. 543-548, 1993.

[12] P.H.S. Torr, D.W. Murray, "A Review of Robust Methods to Estimate the Fundamental Matrix", IJCV, 1997.

[13] P. Pritchett, A. Zisserman, "Wide Baseline Stereo Matching", ICCV, pp. 754-760, 1998.

[14] G. Medioni, Mi-Suen Lee, Chi-Keung Tang, "A Computational Framework for Segmentation and Grouping", Elsevier Science, 2000.

[15] S. Arya, D. Mount, N. Netanyahu, R Silverman, A. Wu, "An Optimal Algorithm for Approximate Nearest Neighbor Searching in Fixed Dimensions", Journal of the ACM, 45:6, pp. 891-923, 1998.

[16] P. Anandan, "A Computational Framework and an Algorithm for the Measurement of Visual Motion", IJCV, vol. 2, pp. 283-310, 1989.

[17] D. McReynolds, D. Lowe, "Rigidity Checking of 3D Point Correspondences Under Perspective Projection", Trans. PAMI, 18(12), pp. 1174-1185, 1996.

[18] D. Scharstein, R. Szeliski, "High-Accuracy Stereo Depth Maps Using Structured Light", CVPR, pp. 195-202, 2003.

Dense Optic Flow with a Bayesian Occlusion Model

Kevin Koeser, Christian Perwass, and Gerald Sommer

Institute of Computer Science and Applied Mathematics,
Christian-Albrechts-University of Kiel,
24098 Kiel, Germany
koeser@mip.informatik.uni-kiel.de
{chp, gs}@ks.informatik.uni-kiel.de

Abstract. This paper presents a dense optic flow algorithm based on quite simple local probability assumptions. Due to the explicit derivation of the correspondence concept in a probability-theoretical framework, occlusion probability evolves straight-forwardly from the model for each pixel. Initialized with a similarity measure based on single pixels, an iterated diffusion step propagates local information across the image, while occlusion probability is used to inhibit flow information transfer across depth discontinuities, which prevents flow smoothing at 3d object boundaries. The inhibition is thereby not artificially modelled by some heuristically chosen parameters, but arises directly from the Bayesian correspondence model. The algorithm structure can be interpreted as a recurrent neural network, where matched points have reached a stable state, while others (e.g. those in homogeneous areas) keep receiving information from regions more and more far away until they converge, this way overcoming the aperture problem. The massive parallel structure allows for and demands a real hardware implementation of the system.

1 Introduction

There are several applications which require a dense displacement field of pixels between images of a video sequence or between different camera images. The efficient and accurate computation of this so-called optical flow especially in presence of occlusion is still an open research topic. Standard dense matchers usually assume some region (a window) around each pixel to be invariant and compare the window of the pixel in image A to all candidate windows in image B to compute a similarity. This creates the problem of finding an appropriate window size, such that the region is significant (aperture problem) but still invariant (regarding occlusion and perspective), which may be avoided in parts if adaptable windows are used [1]. In our approach, there is no need to choose a window size since the region used for matching is automatically extended, when the local information does not suffice for a stable result.

Nearly all proposed optical flow computation methods make use of some kind of smoothness constraint on the flow field as has early been proposed by Horn

W.J. MacLean (Ed.): SCVMA 2004, LNCS 3667, pp. 127–139, 2006.
© Springer-Verlag Berlin Heidelberg 2006

and Schunck [2], where the actual implementation varies, e.g. in Markov Random Field (MRF) approaches [3], nonlinear diffusion [4], global minimization with discontinuity punishment [5] and so on. However, in addition to adding stability to the matching, smoothing also blurs discontinuities in the flow field. Especially at the projections of 3d object boundaries one would like to have a flow field, which is as sharp as possible, such that smoothing has to be avoided in these regions. Most previous Bayesian methods, which have the advantage of making all assumptions explicit (e.g. [6, 7]) did not take occlusion into account yet. When occluded pixels have been considered (as in [8, 9, 4]), they are usually modelled as some additional disturbance of a prior or yield another penalty term in an error function. In our novel approach they are stated in terms of existing probability distributions in the model. Opposed to that in [10], an algorithm for rectified stereo images only, occlusions and discontinuities are modelled by additional stochastic processes with parameters, which have to be estimated simultaneously to the flow in a global optimization scheme. If explicit knowledge about the number of moving objects is present, the computation of boundary curves around regions with uniform displacement may be possible [11], which can then also be used to avoid smoothing at discontinuities. Other techniques directly using high image gradient values for diffusion blocking discard the significant structure for optic flow estimation contained in these regions. In [9] the prior allows discontinuities only at intensity edges, otherwise penalties apply.

The basic concepts of the algorithm used have already been proposed in [12], but occlusion (and the information it carries) has not been taken into account yet. Furthermore, the concept has been extended regarding a scale pyramid initialization, which makes detailed knowledge on pre-positioning obsolete. Initially, the algorithm computes a probability distribution for each pixel in frame 0 among all (predefined) possible match candidates in frame 1 (a test patch) by calculating the probability that both pixels correspond only based on their color. Using only color information of single pixels is usually not enough, such that an additional constraint has to be imposed on the neighborhood. Thus, a local probability measure that demands similar displacement for neighboring pixels is iteratively applied to propagate information throughout the image, such that local constraints are transformed into global information over time. The entropy of the probability distribution among match candidates in the test patches is reduced step-by-step and finally converges to a single (sub-)pixel position, which represents the expected correspondence.

In [4] concepts are comparable to our approach but differ in the implementation of the pixel invariance properties. Where they make use of a MRF to enforce a smooth disparity space, we follow the idea that the distribution of correct pixel matches can locally be described by a particular probability distribution, whereas wrong match candidates are uniformly distributed. Based on our model, we derive that the information propagation (as the equivalent of smoothing) is blocked proportionally to the probability that a pixel is occluded either in the first or in the second image. This helps to improve the matching quality between subsequent frames and sharpens the flow field at depth discontinuities, since moving objects usually introduce occluded pixels into the images.

The occlusion probability is derived straight-forwardly from the Bayesian correspondence theory framework, as opposed to more ad hoc occlusion detection algorithms like "goodness of match discontinuities" or "bimodalities in disparity", which are compared in [13]. Nonetheless, detecting occluded areas is an intricate problem, since they may not exactly coincide with the pixel grid, such that they are smoothed into neighboring pixels. The concept of an occlusion probability accounts perfectly for this. This is an improvement over previous methods, which used a binary distinction between occluded and visible pixels during their minimization scheme [9, 8].

The spread of correspondence information implicitly starts at heavily structured regions, which may be viewed like seed crystals and progresses to homogeneous regions, where the probability distributions converge over time. This may be regarded as automatic feature selection and matching at descriptive points and subsequent guided interpolation across less-structured regions. However, no minimization of a global probability model is carried out, since at each iteration step probabilities are updated with local information only.

The algorithm works on uncalibrated image sequences and is much more scale and rotation tolerant than standard window correlation approaches. It can also be used for (uncalibrated) stereo scenarios and is easily adaptable to exploit the knowledge of rectified epipolar geometry, too. Due to its simple structure a huge number of basic operations is necessary to compute the correspondences, which is well-suited for a parallel implementation using specialized hardware like an FPGA (Field Programmable Gate Array) chip or a graphics card.

2   The Bayesian Model

In the model we develop, we are not interested in the exact camera geometry. We simply assume that we are given two images A and B whose pixels are correlated in as far as they represent the same scene, albeit from a different point of view (stereo matching) or at a different time (optical flow). The only constraints we can invoke then are pixel similarity and an ordering constraint.

We assume that correct matches satisfy a particular statistical distribution whereas incorrect matches are equivalent to noise and are uniformly distributed. We are looking for an iterative procedure that amplifies those pixels that satisfy the appropriate distribution and subdues the others. We can only give a short overview of the algorithm's derivation here. For a detailed account see [14].

First we will derive the local match probabilities, which refer only to the first-order neighborhood of the pixels under inspection. After explaining the concept of correspondence probability, we will finally bind the local probability measures into an iterative algorithm, which increases the region upon which probability statements are based.

2.1   Local Probabilities

The correspondence problem is modelled through random variable pairs (X_A, X_B), where X_A can take on all pixel positions (represented by $\mathcal{I}$) in image A and X_B can take on those in B. However, given some images, these random variables are not independent of one another, we explicitly accept only outcomes of X_A and X_B where the pixel positions $\mathbf{x}_A$ and $\mathbf{x}_B$ both correspond to the same element in 3d space, i.e. the event $(X_A = \mathbf{x}_A, X_B = \mathbf{x}_B)$ means that position $\mathbf{x}_A$ in image A corresponds to $\mathbf{x}_B$ in B. This is our *correspondence pair assumption*, which is implicitly stated in every subsequent probability further down.

To find out which pixels refer to which others, we basically need a measure for pixel similarity. This measure has to express the likelihood that two pixels were created by the same element in a scene, without taking into account any neighboring pixels. Such a measure therefore will be based on a pixel's color, but may also include any other local property like the local scale or local phase. We will denote this measure by $s(a, b)$, where a denotes a pixel color (in image A) and b another color (in image B). A good similarity function is the maximum likelihood estimator as used by Belhumeur in [10].

$$P(A|_{\mathbf{x}_A} = a, B|_{\mathbf{x}_B} = b \mid X_A = \mathbf{x}_A, X_B = \mathbf{x}_B) \simeq s(a, b) \qquad (1)$$

The $\simeq$ here means equality up to a scalar factor, since a pdf must sum to unity. Using $s(A|_{\mathbf{x}_A}, B|_{\mathbf{x}_B})$, we can evaluate for each pixel in image A its similarity to the pixels within an area of image B where we expect the correct match to lie. We will also call this a *test patch* $\mathcal{T}$. Next we scale the computed similarities in $\mathcal{T}$ in a way that they sum to unity, such that we can interpret them as probabilites. That is, each pixel in image A has associated with it a probability distribution giving its matching likelihood to a set of pixels in image B. Our goal is to minimize the entropy of these probability distributions, i.e. to minimize the match uncertainty. In order to do this, the pixel similarity measure alone is not enough. We also have to take into account a structural constraint. We do this by assuming that the local distribution of pixel matches takes on a particular form. This becomes the prior distribution in our derivation, denoted by $h(\mathbf{x}_A, \mathbf{x}_B, \mathbf{y}_A, \mathbf{y}_B)$. That is, given an assumed pixel match $(\mathbf{x}_A, \mathbf{x}_B)$ and a particular neighbor $\mathbf{y}_A$ of $\mathbf{x}_A$, $h(\mathbf{x}_A, \mathbf{x}_B, \mathbf{y}_A, \mathbf{y}_B)$ gives the a priori probability distribution for $\mathbf{y}_B$ being a correct match of $\mathbf{y}_A$. Note that h does not depend

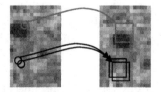

Fig. 1. Left two images: Positions of test patches, right three images: Probability distributions in patches based on pixel similarity

on the images but reflects our assumption that neighboring pixels have a similar displacement. Therefore h yields the highest probabilities if $\mathbf{y}_B$ is chosen such that $\mathbf{x}_A - \mathbf{x}_B = \mathbf{y}_A - \mathbf{y}_B$ and lower values the more the lhs and the rhs of this equation differ. Therefore, a simple choice for h may be a zero-mean Gauss of the difference of lhs and rhs of the above.

$$P(Y_B = \mathbf{y}_B \mid X_A = \mathbf{x}_A, X_B = \mathbf{x}_B, Y_A = \mathbf{y}_A) \simeq h(\mathbf{x}_A, \mathbf{x}_B, \mathbf{y}_A, \mathbf{y}_B) \qquad (2)$$

This is similar to a Gibbs potential as for example used in MRF approaches [3] to describe the preferences of a disparity surface. However, h does not account for all cliques on the disparity surface as in [4] but only for one neighbor.

We are asking how likely it is that $(\mathbf{x}_A, \mathbf{x}_B)$ is a correct match. This depends on the pixel similarity $(s(A|_{\mathbf{x}_A}, B|_{\mathbf{x}_B}))$ and the likelihood that the eight directly neighboring pixels of $\mathbf{x}_A$, denoted by $\{\mathbf{y}_A^i\}$, have high pixel similarities with those pixels in image B $\{\mathbf{y}_B^i\}$ where $h(\mathbf{x}_A, \mathbf{x}_B, \mathbf{y}_A, \mathbf{y}_B)$ is maximal.

Formally, let (X_A, X_B) and (Y_A, Y_B) be the random variables of two neighboring pixel correspondences, i.e. for some $X_A = \mathbf{x}_A$ only outcomes $\mathbf{y}_A$ of Y_A are inspected, where $\mathbf{x}_A$ and $\mathbf{y}_A$ are neighbors and $\mathbf{x}_A$ and $\mathbf{x}_B$ (and also $\mathbf{y}_A$ and $\mathbf{y}_B$) are corresponding pixels. Using Bayes' law together with the s and h functions we get:

$$P(X_B = \mathbf{x}_B, Y_B = \mathbf{y}_B, Y_A = \mathbf{y}_A \mid A, B, X_A = \mathbf{x}_A) \simeq \qquad (3)$$

$$\frac{s(A|_{\mathbf{x}_A}, B|_{\mathbf{x}_B}) s(A|_{\mathbf{y}_A}, B|_{\mathbf{y}_B}) h(\mathbf{x}_B, \mathbf{y}_B, \mathbf{x}_A, \mathbf{y}_A)}{P(X_A = \mathbf{x}_A \mid A, B)}$$

Given some position $\mathbf{x}_A$ in A this equation expresses the probability, that $\mathbf{x}_B$ is the correct match, while the neighbor $\mathbf{y}_A$ of $\mathbf{x}_A$ corresponds to $\mathbf{y}_B$. To make the pdf independent of some particular match candidate $\mathbf{y}_B$, the best matching $\mathbf{y}_B$ (regarding equation (3)) is assumed to be the match of $\mathbf{y}_A$ and its match information is used to evaluate the neighborhood and similarity constraint for $\mathbf{y}_A$. This is in contrast to MRF field methods, which would marginalize at this point over Y_B. We explicitly select only that match candidate for each neighbor, where the image data best satisfies the assumed prior distribution. It was found that this improves convergence. The slightly different pdf is denoted by $\hat{P}$.

Additionally, the match probability for $\mathbf{x}_B$ should also be stated independently of a particular neighbor $\mathbf{y}_A$ of $\mathbf{x}_A$. Therefore we maginalize over all neighbors $\mathbf{y}_A$ and end up with the *pixel-match pdf*:

$$\hat{P}(X_B = \mathbf{x}_B \mid A, B, X_A = \mathbf{x}_A) \simeq$$

$$\frac{s(A|_{\mathbf{x}_A}, B|_{\mathbf{x}_B})}{P(X_A = \mathbf{x}_A \mid A, B)} \cdot \sum_{\mathbf{y}_A:(\mathbf{y}_A - \mathbf{x}_A) \in \mathcal{N}} \max_{\mathbf{y}_B} \left(s(A|_{\mathbf{y}_A}, B|_{\mathbf{y}_B}) h(\mathbf{x}_A, \mathbf{x}_B, \mathbf{y}_A, \mathbf{y}_B) \right) \quad (4)$$

With this equation, we can now compute the probability of each candidate match $\mathbf{x}_B$ in B to be the correct match, given some position $\mathbf{x}_A$ in image A. It is only based on the color and the fitting of the direct neighbors.

2.2   Occlusion Detection

Now we want to inspect the probability that a pixel really has a correspondence in the other image at all. One finds that this information is carried in the probability distributions $P(X_A \mid A, B)$ and $P(X_B \mid A, B)$. We will refer to them as the *correspondence probabilities*. Remember that $P(X_A = \mathbf{x}_A \mid A, B)$ is the probability that random variable X_A has the outcome $\mathbf{x}_A$ under the correspondence pair assumption. If there is no correspondence, X_A will never have the outcome $\mathbf{x}_A$. On the other hand, if every pixel in the image has exactly one correspondence, X_A will be uniformly distributed.

To unterstand the principle used for occlusion detection, suppose two images are matched. If everything works as expected, the test patches eventually have a strong peak at the correct position. Now suppose that there are some occluded pixels, e.g. a pixel $\mathbf{x}_O$ in A, which has no correspondence in image B. Nevertheless, its test patch may have a high value at some position, say $\mathbf{x}_B$ in B, which represents the most likely match for $\mathbf{x}_O$. However, if $\mathbf{x}_B$ has a true match $\mathbf{x}_A$ in A, $\mathbf{x}_B$'s test patch will most likely be maximal at this position and vice versa. That is, $\mathbf{x}_O$'s position (in the test patch of $\mathbf{x}_B$) has a very low probability. One might say that $\mathbf{x}_O$ chose $\mathbf{x}_B$ as a correspondence partner but does not get support from the inverse direction. Now, the observation that occluded pixels do not get support from the inverse direction is exploited to detect them. Both, the lhs and the rhs of the following equation represent $P(X_A, X_B \mid A, B)$:

$$P(X_A \mid A, B)P(X_B \mid A, B, X_A) = P(X_B \mid A, B)P(X_A \mid A, B, X_B) \qquad (5)$$

This equation must hold for every single match candidate in the test patch. However, instead of inspecting single correspondences, it is more promising to evaluate all possible matches in the other image at once and thus to get more robust information. Equation (5) is solved for $P(X_A \mid A, B)$ and summed across all candidate pixels (i.e. across $\mathbf{x}_A$'s test patch $\mathcal{T}_{\mathbf{x}_A}$):

$$P(X_A = \mathbf{x}_A \mid A, B) = \frac{\sum_{\mathbf{x}_B \in \mathcal{T}_{\mathbf{x}_A}} P(X_A = \mathbf{x}_A \mid A, B, X_B = \mathbf{x}_B)P(X_B \mid A, B)}{\sum_{\mathbf{x}_B \in \mathcal{T}_{\mathbf{x}_A}} P(X_B = \mathbf{x}_B \mid A, B, X_A = \mathbf{x}_A)}$$

$$(6)$$

Since there is no preference on matching from A to B or from B to A, the same can be applied to the B to A direction analogously. It can be seen that the probability $P(X_A \mid A, B)$ depends on the support of the inverse direction. Unfortunately, it does also depend on the correspondence probability of that direction. Since both probabilities depend on one another, they cannot be calculated explicitly before the start of the algorithm. Instead, each correspondence probability has to be initialized with some value and is updated iteratively utilizing the above equations, which is referred to as the *collection of support*.

We will now give an interpretation of the correspondence probability values for a binary occlusion classification (which may be desired by a high level application). Since $P(X_A = \mathbf{x}_A \mid A, B)$ is a probability (of the event $\mathbf{x}_A$), summing it over all possible $|\mathcal{I}|$ (disjoint) events must yield unity. As pointed out before, if every pixel has a match, $P(X_A \mid A, B)$ must be a uniform distribution with the value $1/|\mathcal{I}|$. If a single pixel $\mathbf{x}_O$ in A is occluded, the true distribution for X_A yields slightly higher values for all pixels having correspondences and zero for $(X_A = \mathbf{x}_O)$. The more occluded pixels exist, the more the correspondence probability for pixels with true matches increases. Accounting for noise and spurious support, a pixel $\mathbf{x}_O$ should therefore only be classified as occluded, if $P(X_A = \mathbf{x}_O \mid A, B) \ll 1/|\mathcal{I}|$.

Intrinsically the correspondence probability is some kind of measure for the support from the inverse direction. Apart from detecting occluded pixels it also yields a low value in case of low similarity (and great uncertainty) for true matches. Hence, it can also be a hint for the confidence in a pixel's match value, indicating how well the pixel and the neighborhood are found in the other image.

2.3 Propagation of Local Constraints

The structural constraint and the pixel-match pdf refer only to direct neighbors of a pixel. Usually more global information is needed for stable matching results, since the aperture problem is very relevant for these small neighborhoods. This section binds the derived equations into an iterative algorithm, where local information propagates throughout the images step by step.

The previously derived pdf (4) is used as the base equation, where the match probability resulting from the last iteration is used as the pixel similarity for the next round. To abstract from the s-function, f^t is defined to contain the similarities from the tth iteration, where the first f is the similarity s. The functions c_A and c_B represent the correspondence probabilities for the pixels at each iteration (initialized with their expectation value).

$$f^0(\mathbf{x}_A, \mathbf{x}_B) := s(A|_{\mathbf{x}_A}, B|_{\mathbf{x}_B}) \qquad c_A^0(\mathbf{x}_A) := 1/|\mathcal{I}| \qquad c_B^0(\mathbf{x}_B) := 1/|\mathcal{I}|$$

Let $\mathcal{F}^t$ contain the information available at iteration t, i.e. f^t, c_A^t and c_B^t. The resulting pdf $\hat{P}(X_B = \mathbf{x}_B \mid \mathcal{F}^t, X_A = \mathbf{x}_A)$ can then be computed up to scale as:

$$\frac{f^t(\mathbf{x}_A, \mathbf{x}_B)}{c_A^t(\mathbf{x}_A)} \sum_{\mathbf{y}_A:(\mathbf{y}_A-\mathbf{x}_A)\in\mathcal{N}} \max_{\mathbf{y}_B\in\mathcal{T}_{\mathbf{y}_A}} \left(f^t(\mathbf{y}_A, \mathbf{y}_B)h(\mathbf{x}_A, \mathbf{x}_B, \mathbf{y}_A, \mathbf{y}_B)\right) \qquad (7)$$

The correspondence probabilities are computed as described in equation (6):

$$c_A^{t+1}(\mathbf{x}_A) = \hat{P}(X_A = \mathbf{x}_A \mid \mathcal{F}^t) \simeq \frac{\sum_{\mathbf{x}_B\in\mathcal{T}_{\mathbf{x}_A}} \hat{P}(X_A = \mathbf{x}_A \mid \mathcal{F}^t, X_B = \mathbf{x}_B)c_B^t(\mathbf{x}_B)}{\sum_{\mathbf{x}_B\in\mathcal{T}_{\mathbf{x}_A}} \hat{P}(X_B = \mathbf{x}_B \mid \mathcal{F}^t, X_A = \mathbf{x}_A)}$$

$$(8)$$

To get an idea of the final step, imagine first that we directly reuse the probabilities of the last iteration:

$$f^{t+1}(\mathbf{y}_A, \mathbf{y}_B) = \hat{P}(Y_A, Y_B \mid \mathcal{F}^t) \simeq \hat{P}(Y_B = \mathbf{y}_B \mid \mathcal{F}^t, Y_A = \mathbf{y}_A)c_A^t(\mathbf{y}_A) \qquad (9)$$

Using this in equation (7), the term $c_A^t(\mathbf{y}_A)$ is independent of the maximization and may be moved in front of it. It is plain to see that all eight neighbours of

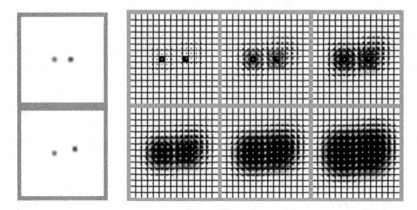

Fig. 2. Upper left: image A, lower left: image B, where blue (right) pixel is moved one pixel right and one up. Right images: Initial test patches (similarity) and first five iterations. At first, test patches in homogeneous regions hold uniform distributions, while those of the red and the blue pixel have already converged to a single position. The neighboring patches have only excluded some candidates. When iterating, more and more candidates becomes improbable, and information propagates throughout the image. However, for the white pixels in between the colored ones, two maxima survive, since it is not clear how they have behaved. The expectation value yields a subpixel position in between the two possible movements.

$\mathbf{x}_A$ are weighted by their correspondence probability c^t, i.e. occluded pixels have a smaller weight than pixels with support. Consequently, the probability for $\mathbf{x}_A$ mainly depends on the probabilities of its not-occluded neighbors.

For stability reasons the simple step of equation (9) is replaced by a bidirectional merging step, because instead of matching from A to B we may also match from B to A as well. Since $P(X_A \mid A, B)P(X_B \mid A, B, X_A)$ and $P(X_B \mid A, B)P(X_A \mid A, B, X_B)$ both represent the same joint probability, they should be equal then. Therefore, we assign their (geometric) average to both of them for the next iteration. Again, this applies only up to scale, since we have to normalize the test patches afterwards. For each patch we choose the factor which makes it sum to unity. Note that the feature of diffusion control by the correspondence probability is not affected by the bidirectional merging.

$$f^{t+1}(\mathbf{x}_A, \mathbf{x}_B) = \hat{P}(X_A, X_B \mid \mathcal{F}^t) \simeq \qquad (10)$$

$$\sqrt{\hat{P}(X_A = \mathbf{x}_A \mid \mathcal{F}^t, X_B = \mathbf{x}_B)c_B^t(\mathbf{x}_B)\hat{P}(X_B = \mathbf{x}_B \mid \mathcal{F}^t, X_A = \mathbf{x}_A)c_A^t(\mathbf{x}_A)}$$

To support large disparities and to detect occlusions at larger scales, the whole process is done using a Gauss pyramid. Starting at the highest layer (usually with image size in the order of 32) images are matched with a test patch size of 5x5 pixels. The pyramid layer and the test patch size encode the maximum displacement expected between the images. For optic flow sequences it is usually sufficient to go up one or two layers, since displacements are in the range of a few pixels. Having calculated the test patches and correspondence probabilities of one layer, test patches of the lower scale are positioned at the interpolated expectation values of the higher ones and correspondence probability is also interpolated from that scale. The matching and occlusion detection is then started for the lower pyramid layer. Depending on the images, after about 10-20 iterations all test patches have converged and the procedure can be repeated with the next layer until finally the original images are matched.

3   Experiments

Though the algorithm allows for a hardware implementation, it has been realized in software for qualitative analysis. Since all operations that may be executed in parallel have to be serialized using a standard CPU, the matching is very slow and takes several minutes. However, an FPGA implementation of a simplified version of the basic algorithm has shown that if enough hardware resources are available, the parallel structure can be exploited to increase speed by several orders of magnitude. To check how the model works in practice, some artificial images with exact ground truth data are evaluated as a first proof of concept in figure (3). To generate image A, a small image is inserted into a large one at a position near the center, simulating a rectangular object, which hides parts of the background. In image B, the foreground object is moved by two pixels to the right and one up, so that it hides a slightly different area of the background.

For evaluation purposes only the A to B direction displacement images are shown, but all observations are also valid for the B to A direction. Setting all correspondence probabilities to constant values (as assumed in [12]) instead of computing them (see figure (4)), most pixels are matched correctly (test patch size 5x3, 20 iterations), but problems occur at the borders of the foreground object. Background pixels left to it and below it are matched badly, although they have well-defined correspondences in the other image. As pointed out, occluded pixels (right of and above the foreground object) have no correspondences, so their match values are neglected here. The displacement field has been smoothed at the left and lower object boundary: Pixels of the background have been strongly influenced by foreground object pixels and are matched as if they were moving

Fig. 3. Artificial flow sequence images (noisy images) generated by moving a 8x16 pixel block (foreground object) by 2 pixels right and one up in front of a 32x32 pixel image (containing uniformly distributed noise,pixelwise independent). Ground truth optical flow is displayed right of each image, i.e. black pixels have the same position in both images, grey ones are displaced. Pure white pixels are occluded in the other image.

Fig. 4. Left two images: A to B results for disabled occlusion detection: Disparity (left), error (right). Pixels above and to the right of the foreground object are occluded in that direction and therefore disregarded in the error analysis. Middle two images: A to B results using correspondence probability: Disparity (left), error (right). Right two images: Correspondence probability. A to B (left) and B to A (right), black pixels mean low values (probably occluded).

with the object. This occurs due to the structural constraint, that demands similar displacements for neighboring pixels. Since there is a very high degree of information and pixel color differs noticably for wrong match candidates, pixels should be matchable quite uniquely. However, without occlusion information, neighboring pixels belonging to a different object are trusted exactly as much as really neighboring pixels are. The matching error is high in these border regions, as can be seen in the error image in the left part of figure (4).

Now the correspondence probability is concurrently computed using the same parameters as before on the same images. The images show the probabilities that some pixel in A has a correspondence in B (left image) and vice versa (right image). All occluded pixels have been detected, i.e. their correspondence probabilities are low. The implications of correct occlusion detection on the matching result can be seen right in figure (4). There are sharp displacement field discontinuities at the object's lower and left borders. The other borders are not relevant for this matching direction since the pixels right and on top of the foreground object in A are occluded in B.

At first sight it is somewhat surprising that the matching results have improved for the A to B direction in regions where there are actually no occluded pixels in that direction, whose influence could have been reduced. This is achieved by bidirectional merging. Occlusions from the other direction discouple the flow field and optimize the matching accuracy of this direction, too.

Adding some noise to image A and image B independently does not disturb the matching results and occlusion detection as can be seen in table (1). Viewing the mean matching error in thousandths can give approximately the number of pixels being matched really wrong. Note that the images used have two artificial properties, which are not always valid for natural images: First, there is very strong structure present, which simplifies the matching and the occlusion detection. Usually natural images are smoother and contain regions with low contrast. Secondly, there are no subpixel correspondences, i.e. no probabilities are distributed across some neighboring pixels and there is a one-to-one correspondence. However, in that scenario, occlusion detection works and improves matching results at image borders, even in the presence of noise.

An interesting approach for the evaluation of optic flow algorithms is used in [15], where a ray-tracer is used to render semi-artificial scenes that look more

Table 1. Mean matching error in presence of Gaussian noise (in percent of the dynamic range of the pixel values) added independently to both images

Noise Level	disabled occl. detection e_M / $\frac{1}{1000}$	enabled occl. detection e_M / $\frac{1}{1000}$
0 %	34.1	1.6
3 %	34.3	1.7
5 %	34.3	1.7
10 %	36.3	1.6

Table 2. Results for the street scene: basic algorithm without occlusion detection(left column), enabled occlusion detection and flow constraint(middle), values of comparing paper(right). $\bar{e}_m$ is the mean absolute error and $\bar{e}_{ma}$ is the mean absolute error in direction orthogonal to the local gradient.

	Simple	Extended	Value Range from [15]
$\bar{e}_m$	0.27	0.21	0.16 .. 0.45
$\bar{e}_{ma}$	0.17	0.13	0.11 .. 0.48

realistic than line patterns or random dot images, but for which full ground truth is provided. We have made experiments on the street sequence from [15], which are quite promising. To exploit the fact that in dense image sequences only small changes apply, we incorporated four frames into the similarity function instead of two. Additionally to using frame 1 and 2 we extrapolate a pixel position in frame 0 and 3 and use their similarities (with smaller weights) as well. This is a preliminary solution, a better way to exploit dense frames may be the use of a Kalman or Particle Filter over time and should be subject to future research. The mean errors are calculated taking into account all images of the sequence and can be seen in table (2) as well as the error range from [15]. The algorithm performs quite well compared to other optic flow algorithms used for this sequence regarding the mean error e_m, again, occlusion information improves the matching result. McCane et al. state that the value e_{ma}, which is quite low here, can give a hint about how well the algorithm can cope with the aperture problem. This value refers only to the first order neighborhood of some pixel and does not depend on the absolute value of the gradient. However, regarding that measure the algorithm can handle the aperture problem quite well, since the error vectors do not always point into the locally most uncertain direction.

The next example shows the results of the aerial Pentagon pair provided by CMU/VASC. Note that the exploitation of the epipolar geometry is only that the test patch height can be set to one. Apart from that the images are handled as if they were two frames of a video sequence.

As pointed out before, white pixels (in the middle images of figure (5)) mean great correspondence probability while black pixels mean low support and thus indicate occluded pixels. Note that the main occlusion lines are detected, but that these lines are not absolutely accurate and sharp. Hence, the matching results are also not sharpened as much as it may have been expected. For completeness reasons the matching results are displayed in the disparity image of figure (5),

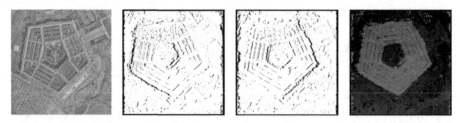

Fig. 5. Aerial image from the CMU/VASC Pentagon pair (left), correspondence probability (middle images) and absolute value of optic flow (right)

Fig. 6. Image of Tsukuba stereo pair, correspondence probability, computed disparity

although this example is intended to demonstrate the occlusion detection in real images. Since there is no real ground truth available for this image pair, it is not exactly known, where the occlusions are and how they look like. If a bird flies over the building or some tree is moving in the wind, occlusion changes. However, the detected occlusions refering to the building look pretty realistic.

In figure (6) the well known Tsukuba pair is displayed. The correspondence probability images show that the algorithm can extract occluded pixels even in real images with (partly) weak structure beneath object borders. Though these probability images are quite noisy, the main occlusions can be seen well. It is also interesting to see that the correspondence probability image is black at the left image border, which is no error due to border problems. Quite the reverse, these pixels are also occluded in the other image, since they have no correspondence there.The disparity image of figure (6) shows a good matching result compared to the ground truth image. The scale approach has positioned the test patches well and the depth discontinuities are represented in the disparity image.

4   Conclusion

A dense matching algorithm has been proposed, which is based on explicit assumptions about local probability distributions in the images. The algorithm extracts occlusion probability for each pixel, which is used in the model to steer the diffusion process. We have shown that this increases the matching quality significantly at depth discontinuities. The algorithm works for uncalibrated cameras and supports a wide range of displacements, since it matches and detects occlusion over a scale pyramid. No explicit window size parameter is needed since the aperture problem is handled automatically by information propagation from structured to homogeneous regions over time, which can be interpreted as a recurrent neural network converging to a stable state. Due to its fundamentally parallel structure, a fast hardware implementation is necessary, which has not been done so far. Another focus of future research must be the exploitation of multiple frames to stabilize the matching and occlusion extraction process.

References

1. Kanade, T., Okutomi, M.: A stereo matching algorithm with an adaptive window: Theory and experiment. IEEE Transactions on PAMI **16** (1994) 920–932
2. Horn, B., Schunck, B.: Determining optical flow. AI **17** (1981) 185–204
3. Marroquin, J., Velasco, F., Rivera, M., Nakamura, M.: Gauss-markov measure field models for low-level vision. IEEE Transactions on PAMI **23** (2001) 337–348
4. Scharstein, D., Szeliski, R.: Stereo matching with nonlinear diffusion. International Journal of Computer Vision **28** (1998) 155–174
5. Zitnick, C., Kanade, T.: A cooperative algorithm for stereo matching and occlusion detection. IEEE Transactions on PAMI **22** (2000) 675–684
6. Vasconcelos, N., Lippman, A.: Empirical bayesian motion segmentation. IEEE Transactions on PAMI **23** (2001) 217–221
7. Torr, P., Szeliski, R., Anandan, P.: An integrated bayesian approach to layer extraction from image sequences. IEEE Transactions on PAMI **23** (2001) 297–303
8. Black, M., Rangarajan, A.: On the unification of line processes, outlier rejection, and robust statistics with applications in early vision. IJCV **19(1)** (1996) 57–91
9. Konrad, J., Dubois, E.: Bayesian estimation of motion vector fields. IEEE Transactions on PAMI **14** (1992) 910–927
10. Belhumeur, P.N.: A Bayesian approach to binocular stereopsis. International Journal of Computer Vision **19** (1996) 237–262
11. Memin, E., Perez, P.: Dense estimation and object-based segmentation of the optical flow with robust techniques. IEEE Transactions on IP **7** (1998) 703–719
12. Perwass, C., Sommer, G.: An iterative bayesian technique for dense image point matching. In: Proceedings of Dynamic Perception. (2002) 283–288
13. Egnal, G., Wildes, R.: Detecting binocular half-occlusions: Empirical comparisons of four approaches. In: IEEE Conference CVPR. (2000) 466–473
14. Koeser, K.: Dense image point matching with explicit occlusion detection for stereo disparity and optic flow. Master's thesis, CAU Kiel (2003) (available at http://www.ks.informatik.uni-kiel.de)
15. Galvin, B., McCane, B., Novins, K., Mason, D., Mills, S.: Recovering motion fields: An evaluation of eight optical flow algorithms. In: Proc. of BMVC. (1998) 195–204

Author Index

Lecture Notes in Computer Science

For information about Vols. 1–3821

please contact your bookseller or Springer

Vol. 3870: S. Spaccapietra, P. Atzeni, W.W. Chu, T. Catarci, K.P. Sycara (Eds.), Journal on Data Semantics V. XIII, 237 pages. 2006.

Vol. 3869: S. Renals, S. Bengio (Eds.), Machine Learning for Multimodal Interaction. XIII, 490 pages. 2006.

Vol. 3868: K. Römer, H. Karl, F. Mattern (Eds.), Wireless Sensor Networks. XI, 342 pages. 2006.

Vol. 3866: T. Dimitrakos, F. Martinelli, P.Y.A. Ryan, S. Schneider (Eds.), Formal Aspects in Security and Trust. X, 259 pages. 2006.

Vol. 3865: W. Shen, K.-M. Chao, Z. Lin, J.-P.A. Barthès (Eds.), Computer Supported Cooperative Work in Design II. XII, 359 pages. 2006.

Vol. 3863: M. Kohlhase (Ed.), Mathematical Knowledge Management. XI, 405 pages. 2006. (Sublibrary LNAI).

Vol. 3862: R.H. Bordini, M. Dastani, J. Dix, A.E.F. Seghrouchni (Eds.), Programming Multi-Agent Systems. XIV, 267 pages. 2006. (Sublibrary LNAI).

Vol. 3861: J. Dix, S.J. Hegner (Eds.), Foundations of Information and Knowledge Systems. X, 331 pages. 2006.

Vol. 3860: D. Pointcheval (Ed.), Topics in Cryptology – CT-RSA 2006. XI, 365 pages. 2006.

Vol. 3858: A. Valdes, D. Zamboni (Eds.), Recent Advances in Intrusion Detection. X, 351 pages. 2006.

Vol. 3857: M.P.C. Fossorier, H. Imai, S. Lin, A. Poli (Eds.), Applied Algebra, Algebraic Algorithms and Error-Correcting Codes. XI, 350 pages. 2006.

Vol. 3855: E. A. Emerson, K.S. Namjoshi (Eds.), Verification, Model Checking, and Abstract Interpretation. XI, 443 pages. 2005.

Vol. 3854: I. Stavrakakis, M. Smirnov (Eds.), Autonomic Communication. XIII, 303 pages. 2006.

Vol. 3853: A.J. Ijspeert, T. Masuzawa, S. Kusumoto (Eds.), Biologically Inspired Approaches to Advanced Information Technology. XIV, 388 pages. 2006.

Vol. 3852: P.J. Narayanan, S.K. Nayar, H.-Y. Shum (Eds.), Computer Vision – ACCV 2006, Part II. XXXI, 977 pages. 2006.

Vol. 3851: P.J. Narayanan, S.K. Nayar, H.-Y. Shum (Eds.), Computer Vision – ACCV 2006, Part I. XXXI, 973 pages. 2006.

Vol. 3850: R. Freund, G. Păun, G. Rozenberg, A. Salomaa (Eds.), Membrane Computing. IX, 371 pages. 2006.

Vol. 3849: I. Bloch, A. Petrosino, A.G.B. Tettamanzi (Eds.), Fuzzy Logic and Applications. XIV, 438 pages. 2006. (Sublibrary LNAI).

Vol. 3848: J.-F. Boulicaut, L. De Raedt, H. Mannila (Eds.), Constraint-Based Mining and Inductive Databases. X, 401 pages. 2006. (Sublibrary LNAI).

Vol. 3847: K.P. Jantke, A. Lunzer, N. Spyratos, Y. Tanaka (Eds.), Federation over the Web. X, 215 pages. 2006. (Sublibrary LNAI).

Vol. 3846: H. J. van den Herik, Y. Björnsson, N.S. Netanyahu (Eds.), Computers and Games. XIV, 333 pages. 2006.

Vol. 3845: J. Farré, I. Litovsky, S. Schmitz (Eds.), Implementation and Application of Automata. XIII, 360 pages. 2006.

Vol. 3844: J.-M. Bruel (Ed.), Satellite Events at the MoDELS 2005 Conference. XIII, 360 pages. 2006.

Vol. 3843: P. Healy, N.S. Nikolov (Eds.), Graph Drawing. XVII, 536 pages. 2006.

Vol. 3842: H.T. Shen, J. Li, M. Li, J. Ni, W. Wang (Eds.), Advanced Web and Network Technologies, and Applications. XXVII, 1057 pages. 2006.

Vol. 3841: X. Zhou, J. Li, H.T. Shen, M. Kitsuregawa, Y. Zhang (Eds.), Frontiers of WWW Research and Development - APWeb 2006. XXIV, 1223 pages. 2006.

Vol. 3840: M. Li, B. Boehm, L.J. Osterweil (Eds.), Unifying the Software Process Spectrum. XVI, 522 pages. 2006.

Vol. 3839: J.-C. Filliâtre, C. Paulin-Mohring, B. Werner (Eds.), Types for Proofs and Programs. VIII, 275 pages. 2006.

Vol. 3838: A. Middeldorp, V. van Oostrom, F. van Raamsdonk, R. de Vrijer (Eds.), Processes, Terms and Cycles: Steps on the Road to Infinity. XVIII, 639 pages. 2005.

Vol. 3837: K. Cho, P. Jacquet (Eds.), Technologies for Advanced Heterogeneous Networks. IX, 307 pages. 2005.

Vol. 3836: J.-M. Pierson (Ed.), Data Management in Grids. X, 143 pages. 2006.

Vol. 3835: G. Sutcliffe, A. Voronkov (Eds.), Logic for Programming, Artificial Intelligence, and Reasoning. XIV, 744 pages. 2005. (Sublibrary LNAI).

Vol. 3834: D.G. Feitelson, E. Frachtenberg, L. Rudolph, U. Schwiegelshohn (Eds.), Job Scheduling Strategies for Parallel Processing. VIII, 283 pages. 2005.

Vol. 3833: K.-J. Li, C. Vangenot (Eds.), Web and Wireless Geographical Information Systems. XI, 309 pages. 2005.

Vol. 3832: D. Zhang, A.K. Jain (Eds.), Advances in Biometrics. XX, 796 pages. 2005.

Vol. 3831: J. Wiedermann, G. Tel, J. Pokorný, M. Bieliková, J. Štuller (Eds.), SOFSEM 2006: Theory and Practice of Computer Science. XV, 576 pages. 2006.

Vol. 3830: D. Weyns, H. V.D. Parunak, F. Michel (Eds.), Environments for Multi-Agent Systems II. VIII, 291 pages. 2006. (Sublibrary LNAI).

Vol. 3829: P. Pettersson, W. Yi (Eds.), Formal Modeling and Analysis of Timed Systems. IX, 305 pages. 2005.

Vol. 3828: X. Deng, Y. Ye (Eds.), Internet and Network Economics. XVII, 1106 pages. 2005.

Vol. 3827: X. Deng, D.-Z. Du (Eds.), Algorithms and Computation. XX, 1190 pages. 2005.

Vol. 3826: B. Benatallah, F. Casati, P. Traverso (Eds.), Service-Oriented Computing - ICSOC 2005. XVIII, 597 pages. 2005.

Vol. 3824: L.T. Yang, M. Amamiya, Z. Liu, M. Guo, F.J. Rammig (Eds.), Embedded and Ubiquitous Computing – EUC 2005. XXIII, 1204 pages. 2005.

Vol. 3823: T. Enokido, L. Yan, B. Xiao, D. Kim, Y. Dai, L.T. Yang (Eds.), Embedded and Ubiquitous Computing – EUC 2005 Workshops. XXXII, 1317 pages. 2005.

Vol. 3822: D. Feng, D. Lin, M. Yung (Eds.), Information Security and Cryptology. XII, 420 pages. 2005.